HOW TO RENT & BUY
PROPERTY IN ITALY

50p

In this Series

Other titles in preparation

RENT & BUY PROPERTY IN ITALY

Amanda Hinton

How To Books

British Library Cataloguing-in-publication data
A catalogue record for this book is available from the British Library.

First published in 1993 by How To Books Ltd, Plymbridge House, Estover
Road, Plymouth PL6 7PZ, United Kingdom. Tel: Plymouth (0752) 735251/
695745. Fax: (0752) 695699. Telex: 45635.

Note: The material contained in this book is set out in good faith for general
guidance and no liability can be accepted for loss or expense incurred as a
result of relying in particular circumstances on statements made in the book.
The laws and regulations are complex and liable to change, and readers
should check the current position with the relevant authorities before making
personal arrangements.

Typeset by Concept Communications (Design & Print) Ltd, Crayford, Kent.
Printed and bound by BPCC Wheatons Ltd, Exeter.

Contents

List of Illustrations

Preface

Renting or buying property in Italy is neither more nor less difficult than in the UK, but the system is different, and therefore it is best to be well-informed before making any decisions or commitments. You will also find that the better informed you are the easier it will be to jump the bureaucratic hurdles that will inevitably present themselves.

At the same time as adjusting to a new system you will also be changing your lifestyle, as Italian homes are tailored to Italian lifestyles and to the Italian climate. If you are moving into a house you will probably find you will live on the first floor, which avoids the problem of damp. The ground floor is generally used as garage space and storage. Bathrooms will all have bidets — the Italians regard the British bidetless bathroom with horror — and the windows will all be shuttered, allowing greater control over light and temperature inside the house, especially in summer when it becomes very hot. Floors are generally tiled and so you will have to give up the ubiquitous fitted carpets of British homes, and adapt to the hard beauty of terracotta, ceramic or parquet floors. You may also have to get used to running all your household appliances on a meagre allowance of 3 kw.

This book prepares you for setting up a home in Italy, guiding you through the bureaucratic labyrinth and helping you cope with everyday life, especially with those aspects connected to your Italian property. There is information on all facets of renting and buying, from how to find properties to legal procedures. Those intending to renovate property will find a wealth of practical information, including a guide to the costs involved. Prices are also given for property, land and rents.

I hope you will find this book a useful reference guide, both before you leave and after you arrive in Italy.

Amanda Hinton

Fig. 1. Map of Italy.

1
Property Guide

ITALIAN LIVING

Over the last thirty years standards of living in Italy have changed dramatically, and this is especially evident in housing. As recently as the 1960s, living conditions in many Italian houses were still very basic, particularly in rural districts, where many homes didn't have either a bathroom or toilet. Within the last two decades, however, the Italians have been making up for their poor past, and houses and apartments have been restored, built and furnished to luxury standards that would put the average British house to shame. The home in Italy, like one's car and clothes, is a prestige symbol, and no expense is spared.

OLD RURAL HOUSES

At the bottom of the housing market in Italy are the many rural houses, of differing dimensions, that were gradually abandoned during the post-1945 era and which now lie slowly deteriorating deep in the country. They are often far more than 100 years old and can be located in the most beautiful surroundings. Unfortunately their locations are also very inaccessible, and there may not be any road at all for one or more kilometres. Houses of this type are constructed with stone, usually locally quarried, and roofed with terracotta pantiles in the south and central Italy, and stone or slate in the north. The interior typically has floors of brick, roughly plastered walls, and a beam and brick ceiling.

The ground floor is generally dark, gloomy and damp. It would have been used for animals or for making wine and does not connect with the living space upstairs, to which there is usually an external staircase in southern and central regions. The living area usually has a large central fireplace, which would have been used for both cooking and heating. The property may or may not have a bathroom, running water and electricity, depending on when it was last lived in. Obviously conditions vary considerably from those that need to be rebuilt totally to those that need superficial restoration.

OLD URBAN HOUSES

The urban population was always somewhat wealthier than the rural one and old town houses are large and elegant. It was very common for one extremely big building, a *palazzo*, to be constructed in the form of numerous large apartments, with a communal hall and stairway, and in some cases an internal courtyard or garden. The apartments themselves often have high ceilings decorated with plaster moulding and frescoes and numerous large rooms usually organised in a circular pattern, so that it is possible to move from room to room, eventually arriving back at the starting point. As these buildings have never been abandoned to the extent of those in the country, the basics of a bathroom, water, electricity and gas usually exist. This type of building has often been modified and modernised from time to time throughout its history.

NEW HOUSES

In recent years the most prestigious housing has been the 'villa', a house set in the countryside or the suburbs of a town, with a garden. Built to luxury standards internally, they unfortunately often have rather ugly, or at least bland, exteriors of pastel-painted cement. They seem to have little in common with the housing of the past, or of the local region, except that the basement or ground floor is not generally a living space. Italians still prefer to live on the first floor, using the *cantina* on the ground floor to park cars and store junk. Terracotta floors have given way to high-fired ceramic tiles, parquet or composite marble. Walls and ceilings are neatly plastered and painted, very rarely wallpapered, and most homes have two bathrooms, usually clad in a flashy show of ceramic tiles. Many homes also have two kitchens, as entertaining and family parties are an important part of Italian living, and part of the house, either an attic, or an adjoining annexe where there is a large dining area and a kitchen, is reserved solely for this purpose.

CONDOMINIUMS

In the last thirty years many Italians have chosen to live in condominiums, apartment blocks which contain at least five separately owned flats which share facilities and services. The **condominio** (condominium) is run by an **amministratore** (administrator) who is elected by an **assemblea condominiale** (condominium assembly) which comprises individual proprietors. Each member of the *assemblea condominiale* has the power to vote against or for decisions involving the condominium. The power of the vote depends on the *milecesimale*, the fraction of thousandths which is calculated according to the size of your flat and the number of balconies it has. Ultimately, however, decisions are made by the Italian law which has formulated a very complicated *regolamento* (set of rules), and you will find your *condominio* probably has a set of *regolamento* in line with the current legislation.

Service charges and maintenance fees are among the most important economic factors in living in a condominium. All bills, apart from gas, electricity and water, are divided between the condominium according to the *milecesimale* assigned to each proprietor. The parts of the condominium for which you are responsible as a community are as follows:

- land on which building stands
- foundations of building
- exterior walls
- roof
- solar panels
- stairs
- entrance ways
- porches
- courtyards.

Residents of a condominium are also usually responsible for the following:

- lift or escalator
- water pump, cistern, pipes
- gas installation
- heating installation (when centralised)
- TV installation (when centralised)
- intercom or videointercom
- waste pipes.

All these can add up to hefty and unpredictable charges. The charges are usually payable in two instalments per annum. An approximation is made for the year and divided in two. But if an unforeseen maintenance job is necessary the second instalment can be a nasty shock. Another idiosyncracy of living in a condominium is the heating system. If your condominium has a communal heating boiler then you will find that you will only be able to use your heating in the official heating times which run from October to April and that the temperature may not be very responsive to the different seasonal conditions.

THE PROPERTY MARKET

The Italian property market is dominated by housing for big families who represent 50 per cent of all buyers. Young couples make up 28.7 per cent and the remainder is divided between firms who comprise 10.2 per cent and single people who represent 8.5 per cent. Statistics show that 25 per cent of the buying market purchase properties in historic centres, 34 per cent buy hinterland locations, while 30 per cent purchase property in suburbs and town outskirts. Statistics also show that the property market in general is on the decline. Some of the most keenly felt drops in property values have been in Rome and Milan and in prestigious tourist spots such as Cortina and Courmayeur. For more details on trends in local property markets see the next section, Where and What to Buy.

WHERE AND WHAT TO BUY

Deciding where to settle in Italy can be an exciting and absorbing process. There are many considerations apart from prices: each region has its own distinct character and way of life. Looking at prices in general it is clear that the most expensive properties are in and around the major cities of the north; on the shores of the northern lakes; along the Ligurian coast; in and around the coastal resorts of Amalfi, Sorrento and Capri; and also along the Smeralda coast in Sardinia. Tuscany is also well on the way to joining this league, partly due to the number of properties bought by foreigners, although there is some variation across the region, with some districts being more favoured than others. However, the price of property varies greatly, and general rules are hard to formulate, except perhaps that a town-centre apartment is likely to cost considerably more than the equivalent in the UK, while a ruined barn, or country cottage will probably cost considerably less.

The following property guide may help you in making your decision as to where to settle in Italy. It lists all twenty of Italy's regions in alphabetical order. A few facts about each region are followed by a general introduction to the region's appearance and economy followed by information on trends in local property markets and general property prices. Prices are given in millions of Italian lire and are calculated per square metre. In city properties there are three classifications: *new*, which means less than 10 years old although it can mean an old property that has been modernised and totally restored within the last 10 years; *recent*, which means less than 30 years old; and *old*, which means more than 30 years old. Under coastal properties there are three classifications regarding its position: *detached*, which means it is a property in an isolated and usually scenic setting; *resort*, which means that it is a property in a town or coastal resort; and *periphery*, which means that it is a property on the outskirts of a town or coastal resort. Prices are also given for land in each regional province. This falls under four classifications: *cultivated, uncultivated, meadow* and *forest*. The prices are given in millions of Italian lire per hectare, but are calculated on a purchase of an average plot of land, which is about 15 hectares. However, you should allow leeway of about 15 per cent either side of the minimum and maximum prices.

Abruzzo

Area	10,974 km^2
Population	1,235,060
Inhabitants per km^2	114
Regional capital	L'Aquila
Provincial capitals	L'Aquila, Chieti, Pescara, Teramo
Airports	Pescara, Rome

The Abruzzo region is predominantly hilly and mountainous, being dominated by the Central Appennines which have peaks of up to 2,912 m high. Due to the severity of the terrain, the road network is fairly tortuous, with the good roads centering on L'Aquila. There is also a motorway which crosses the region, running inland from Pescara to Rome. The majority of the region's commerce and its tourist industry is focused on Pescara, although there are a growing number of visitors who are attracted to the Abruzzo National Park in the mountainous heart of the region, for walking during the summer and skiing in winter.

Other industry in the Abruzzo is concentrated on the processing of local agricultural products, namely grains and cereals, but even agriculture is limited due to the poor soils and steep terrain, and much of the upland area is given over to sheep grazing. Cheese derived from the sheep's milk is an important and delicious Abruzzo product. On the more gentle slopes vines and olives are grown, while along the coast potatoes are cultivated

Property prices

Location	Condition	Price
L'Aquila	New	1.7–2.4
Pescara	New	1.6–2.4
Teramo	New	1.2–1.6
Coast	Detached	2.0–2.5
	Resort	1.8–2.2
	Periphery	1.4–1.7

Land prices

Province	Type	Price
L'Aquila	Cultivated	2.5–18.0
	Uncultivated	1.0
	Meadow	2.5–13.0
	Forest	2.0–10.0
Chieti	Cultivated	4.0–20.0
	Uncultivated	1.0–2.0
	Meadow	3.5–4.0
	Forest	4.5–7.0
Pescara	Cultivated	3.0–26.0
	Uncultivated	1.0–2.5
	Meadow	4.0–5.0
	Forest	3.0–11.5
Teramo	Cultivated	6.5–21.0
	Uncultivated	1.0–1.5
	Meadow	4.0–4.5
	Forest	6.0–9.0

Fig. 2. Property and land prices in Abruzzo.

and in the valleys around L'Aquila there is saffron, a product that has been cultivated here since ancient times.

The local architecture is typified by roughly built stone houses with small windows, huddled next to each other on hillsides, while the towns tend to be dominated by rather severe stone *palazzi*.

It is not a popular area either as a holiday resort or as a place to live, partly due to its inaccessibility and its rather bleak climate. The winter in the interior is long and cold, with the mountains retaining their snowy peaks well into the summer. The property market is sluggish and you can expect to pay rock-bottom prices for buildings in need of renovation. Prices on the coast are somewhat more competitive. For an idea of property and land prices see Fig. 2.

Basilicata

Area	9,992 km^2
Population	614,522
Inhabitants per km^2	61
Regional capital	Potenza
Provincial capitals	Potenza, Matera
Airports	Naples, Bari, Brindisi

Basilicata is a mountainous region in which only 8 per cent of the land is suitable for cultivation. Despite this 40 per cent of the work-force are involved in agriculture, working on the smallest parcels of land to be found in Italy. Basilicata has long suffered impoverished conditions, and in recent years it has been tied up with the corruption surrounding the now abandoned *mezzogiorno* scheme for financial aid. In addition, recession has hit the region badly, with factory closures, such as the textile industry in Maratea, being common. The production of crafts for tourism is one of the few local industries that show signs of thriving.

The landscape and local architecture seem to reflect the way of life in the region. Hill villages, many of which are semi-abandoned, are carved into the land and bleached as pale as the surrounding arid soils. The houses are small and many have flat roofs or very shallow pitched roofs with sun-parched terracotta tiles. The region also has a lot of poorly built modern housing blocks which invariably look unfinished even if they are not.

Basilicata is not a popular tourist destination. Matera, with its *sassi*, rock-hewn dwellings, attracts coach parties, but it is a region the tourist passes through with the exception of the very short stretch of coast on the

Property prices		
Location	Condition	Price
Coast	Resort	1.2–1.5
	Periphery	0.9–1.0

Land prices		
Province	Type	Price
Campobasso	Cultivated	3.0–8.5
	Forest	2.0–3.0
Isernia	Cultivated	6.0–16.5
	Forest	4.5–6.0

Fig. 3. Property and land prices in Basilicata.

Property prices		
Location	Condition	Price
Catanzaro	New	0.9–1.0
Coast	Detached	1.1–1.5
	Resort	0.8–1.5
	Periphery	0.9–1.2

Land prices		
Province	Type	Price
Catanzaro	Cultivated	6.0–15.5
	Meadow	2.0–6.5
	Forest	5.0–12.0
Cosenza	Cultivated	5.0–17.0
	Meadow	3.0–9.0
	Forest	4.5–8.5
Reggio Calabria	Cultivated	4.5–12.5
	Meadow	3.5–4.0
	Forest	6.5–17.0

Fig. 4. Property and land prices in Calabria.

Tyrrhenian Sea where there is some dramatic scenery. Basilicata also touches the coast briefly at the Taranto Gulf on the Ionian Sea where the flat coastal plain is densely cultivated with citrus and peach orchards. Some prices for coastal and land property are given in Fig. 3.

Calabria

Area	15,080 km^2
Population	2,098,137
Inhabitants per km^2	139
Regional capital	Catanzaro
Provincial capitals	Catanzaro, Cosenza
Airports	Reggio di Calabria

Calabria, the toe of Italy's boot, is hemmed in by both a railway line and a coastal road, giving good access to all parts of the coast, but it has little in the way of communications in the mountainous interior, which remains virtually inaccessible. The Sila mountains dominate the northern part of the region and the Aspromonte the south, both rising to heights of almost 2,000 m. The southern part of Calabria has some flat land and large fertile plains provide grain for the region, but the area amounts to less than 9 per cent of the total region.

Agriculture is on the decline, although the coasts are still thickly covered with olive groves and citrus orchards, some of which grow bergamot, a product that is exclusive to Calabria. Ugly industrial developments have appeared at many coastal spots, namely Vibo Valentia Marina, Catanzaro Marina and Crotone. Even so, unemployment is high and the income per head is the lowest in Italy. Calabria has always been impoverished and the tough conditions in the region gave rise to mass emigration in the 1960s and 1970s.

Tourism is one aspect of the Calabrian economy that is on the upturn. There are many fine spots along its extensive coastline although, apart from the headland at Tropea, there is always the railway and road to cross. Generally, new costal properties are not built to the same standard as in other regions and may make undesirable investments. The coast was never inhabited much in the past due to its vulnerability to attack, so almost the only old buildings you will see are defensive coastal towers. However, the hinterland holds many attractive old hill villages built of a greyish colour stone with terracotta roofs.

Prices for land and coastal property are given in Fig. 4 (page 18).

Campania

Area	13,595 km^2
Population	5,563,230
Inhabitants per km^2	409
Regional capital	Naples
Provincial capitals	Naples, Avellino, Benevento, Caserta, Salerno
Airports	Naples

Just under a quarter of Campania's population live in and around Naples, which is choked by industrial developments as is Salerno. Despite the dominance of industry, agriculture, especially the cultivation of tomatoes, is also an important element of the local economy, employing as it does 24 per cent of the workforce, although agricultural salaries are well below the national average. In contrast to the poverty of agricultural workers, there are the wealthy hotel owners and restaurateurs who are based in the luxurious tourist resorts, including Amalfi and Sorrento, as well as the offshore island of Capri. The local architecture reflects this state of affairs with small, semi-abandoned stone villages in the steeply rolling hills, and immaculately painted villas and *palazzi* in the resorts along the coast. There is also a good deal of very poor architecture, particularly on the fringes of the main cities, where there is tower after tower of shoddily built apartment blocks.

Property both in Naples and on the prestigious Campanian coast is a valuable asset. Having suffered a slight decline in sales in 1991, stability has returned to the market with prices expected to rise slowly, particularly in Naples where industry is ever expanding. Prices for property in Naples and on the coast and land are given in Fig. 5 (page 21).

Emilia-Romagna

Area	22,122 km^2
Population	3,952,304
Inhabitants per km^2	179
Regional capital	Bologna
Provincial capitals	Bologna, Ferrara, Forli, Modena, Parma, Piacenza, Ravenna, Reggio nell'Emilia
Airports	Rimini, Ravenna, Forli, Bologna

Emilia Romagna is a flat, intensely cultivated region with at least half of

Property prices		
Location	*Condition*	*Price*
Naples (centre)	New	1.8–5.2
	Recent	1.0–3.8
	Old	0.7–3.1
Avellino	New	1.5–1.9
Benevento	New	1.7–2.1
Salerno	New	2.2–4.0
Coast	Detached	3.0–10.0
	Resort	3.0–8.0
	Periphery	2.8–6.0

Land prices		
Province	*Type*	*Price*
Avellino	Cultivated	7.0–27.0
	Uncultivated	2.5–4.0
	Meadow	5.5–8.5
	Forest	5.0–6.5
Benevento	Cultivated	11.5–22.5
	Uncultivated	2.5–3.5
	Meadow	8.0–15.0
	Forest	8.0–11.5
Caserta	Cultivated	25.0–58.5
	Uncultivated	3.5–8.0
	Meadow	18.0–27.5
	Forest	7.5–13.5
Napoli	Cultivated	27.0–59.5
	Uncultivated	2.5–7.5
	Meadow	16.0–21.5
	Forest	12.0–15.0
Salerno	Cultivated	5.0–6.0
	Meadow	5.5–28
	Forest	7.0–11.0

Fig. 5. Property and land prices in Campania.

the land given over to large-scale farming. It is Italy's number one producer of grain, sugar beet and fruits such as apricot, cherry and peach. It is also important for the cultivation of tomatoes, vines and rice. The flat, monotonous landscape is criss-crossed by numerous major rivers including the Po. Many of the rivers empty into the Adriatic where the flat Emilia-Romagna coast is edged by sandy beaches and extensive areas of reclaimed land.

The region is also well endowed with industry, having many large towns with even larger industrial outskirts. These towns mostly have attractive historic centres, with arcaded streets and brick *palazzi* centring on the ubiquitous cobbled piazza and its neatly restored cathedral. Country properties tend to be prestigious estates with neat red-roofed farmhouses. Many farms are involved in the production of cheeses, cured hams and salamis which are well-known throughout Italy, while Parma claims international fame for its ham and parmesan.

Emilia-Romagna is a region where people live and work but strive to escape from in the holiday periods. Due to the general affluence of the region, property prices are quite high. In Bologna the current trend in the property market is for a gradual increase in both sales and prices. In 1992 there was a 2 per cent increase in sales in the historic centre, a 14.3 per cent increase in suburban sales, and a 27.5 per cent rise in sales in outer-city areas. Most of the large towns in Emilia-Romagna have similar statistics. It is probably not the region in which to look for a derelict property at a give-away price. For some idea of the going rates in Emilia-Romagna see Fig. 6 (page 23).

Friuli-Venezia Giulia

Area	7,846 km^2
Population	1,228,180
Inhabitants per km^2	157
Regional capital	Trieste
Provincial capitals	Trieste, Gorizia, Pordenone, Udine
Airports	Venice

The small, semi-autonomous region of Friuli-Venezia Giulia is made up of the snow-capped Alps which form the border with Austria in the north, rolling vine-covered hills in the centre and flat alluvial plains that extend to the Adriatic coast in the south. The mountains, which have peaks well over 2,500m, provide pasture lands for sheep, while the plains are intensely cultivated with grain and fruit orchards. Industry has built up around

Property prices

Location	Condition	Price
Bologna	New	3.5–7.0
	Recent	2.5–5.5
	Old	1.8–3.0
Ferrara	New	1.7–2.1
Forli	New	1.5–1.7
Modena	New	2.2–2.4
Parma	New	2.1–3.5
Piacenza	New	1.7–2.5
Ravenna	New	1.6–2.0
Reggio Emilia	New	1.6–3.2
Coast	Detached	1.3–4.8
	Resort	1.1–4.4
	Periphery	1.1–4.2

Fig. 6. Property and land prices in Emilia-Romagna.

Land prices

Province	Type	Price
Bologna	Cultivated	6.5–33.0
	Uncultivated	1.5–8.0
	Meadow	4.0–12.0
	Forest	6.0–7.0
Ferrara	Cultivated	23.0–30.0
	Uncultivated	6.0–15.0
	Meadow	15.0–20.0
	Forest	14.0
Forli	Cultivated	4.5–24.5
	Uncultivated	2.0–2.5
	Meadow	2.5–8.5
	Forest	4.0–11.0
Modena	Cultivated	7.0–29.0
	Uncultivated	2.5–3.5
	Meadow	4.5–20.0
	Forest	7.5–15.0
Parma	Cultivated	6.5–28.0
	Uncultivated	1.5–2.5
	Meadow	3.5–13.0
	Forest	5.5–9.5
Piacenza	Cultivated	5.0–28.5
	Uncultivated	1.0–2.0
	Meadow	3.0–28.0
	Forest	6.0–14.0
Ravenna	Cultivated	8.5–25.5
	Uncultivated	3.0–8.0
	Meadow	4.0–12.0
	Forest	7.0–16.5
Reggio Emilia	Cultivated	3.5–26.5
	Uncultivated	—
	Meadow	3.5–6.5
	Forest	2.5–5.5

Fig. 6. Continued.

	Property price	
Location	Condition	Price
Trieste	New	2.5–3.0
	Recent	1.3–2.5
	Old	0.9–1.5
Gorizia	New	1.5–1.7
Pordenone	New	1.2–1.7
Udine	New	1.8–2.3
Coast	Detached	2.5–3.5
	Resort	2.0–7.0
	Periphery	1.0–1.5
Mountains	Detached	1.8–2.0
	Resort	1.5–1.8
	Periphery	1.6–2.0
	Land prices	
Province	Type	Price
Gorizia	Cultivated	23.0–25.5
	Uncultivated	—
	Meadow	15.0–17.0
	Forest	10.0–11.5
Pordenone	Cultivated	16.5–30.5
	Uncultivated	—
	Meadow	9.0–12.5
	Forest	—
Trieste	Cultivated	62.0
	Uncultivated	—
	Meadow	40.0
	Forest	—
Udine	Cultivated	21.0–25.0
	Uncultivated	—
	Meadow	8.0–15.0
	Forest	11.0–12.5

Fig. 7. Property and land prices in Friuli-Venezia Giulia

all four of the provincial capitals with a refinery and one of the most important commercial ports on the Adriatic at Trieste which is within a stone's throw of what was once Yugoslavia.

The coast, dotted with lagoons and marshes, is not a popular tourist destination, with the exception of the resort of Grado, although the mountain resorts attract a certain number of holiday-makers. Generally the region is avoided because of its cold damp winters. Property is reasonably priced and attractive Venetian architecture dominates many of the towns. In the mountains there are well-built chalets of stone with slate roofs, and on the coast, particularly on the Lagoon of Marano, you will find traditional fisherman's houses built of reeds with cone-shaped roofs.

For an idea of the going prices in the region see Fig. 7 (page 25).

Lazio

Area	17,203 km^2
Population	5,056,119
Inhabitants per km^2	294
Regional capital	Rome
Provincial capitals	Rome, Frosinone, Latina, Rieti, Viterbo
Airports	Rome

The region of Lazio has a central position, touching all five regions of central Italy as well as Campania, and it is criss-crossed by a good road network. The countryside is characterised by pretty rolling hills, dotted with gracious villas, stone-walled towns, vineyards and olive groves. There are also a great number of hazelnut orchards, Lazio being the second largest producer of hazelnuts in Italy. Agriculture plays an important role in Lazio's economy despite the growing industry that surrounds Rome and stretches southwards to Latina.

The architecture of Lazio is typified by the many fortified hill towns, which are built of a greyish stone and which contain tall, thin houses. Prices for property in Lazio's hill towns are high; the same is true for property on the palm-lined coast from where Romans either commute or have their weekend retreats. Surprisingly, however, property prices in Rome itself are falling. 1992 saw a sales decrease of 27 per cent while prices have remained static, except for prestigious city centre properties. Agents do not expect this trend to change in the foreseeable future. A guide to property and land prices is given in Fig. 8 (page 27).

Property prices

Location	Condition	Price
Rome (centre)	New	3.5–17.0
	Recent	3.0–15.0
	Old	2.7–13.5
Latina	New	1.7–1.8
Rieti	New	1.3–1.8
Viterbo	New	1.6–2.2
Coast	Detached	2.0–4.5
	Resort	2.0–4.5
	Periphery	1.5–3.0

Land prices

Province	Type	Price
Frosinone	Cultivated	6.5–11.0
	Uncultivated	2.0–2.5
	Meadow	7.0–10.0
	Forest	4.5–7.5
Latina	Cultivated	6.0–20.5
	Uncultivated	2.0–2.5
	Meadow	5.0–13.5
	Forest	5.0–10.5
Rieti	Cultivated	3.5–10.0
	Uncultivated	1.0–2.0
	Meadow	4.5–6.5
	Forest	4.5–7.5
Rome	Cultivated	6.0–25.0
	Uncultivated	2.0–4.0
	Meadow	3.5–26.5
	Forest	4.5–11.5
Viterbo	Cultivated	7.5–12.5
	Uncultivated	2.5–4.5
	Meadow	5.0–9.5
	Forest	7.0–8.0

Fig. 8. Property and land prices in Lazio

Liguria

Area:	5,415 km^2
Population	1,789,225
Inhabitants per km^2	330
Regional capital	Genoa
Provincial capitals	Genoa, Imperia, La Spezia, Savona
Airports	Genoa, Pisa

Liguria is one of the smallest regions in Italy. It is dominated by the Ligurian Apennines and Maritime Alps which sweep up from the Tyrrhenian leaving only a narrow but very beautiful coastal strip. The coast has been a popular holiday destination ever since the British started coming here in the 1920s.

The Côte d'Azur, which is a continuation of the Ligurian coast, is probably more fashionable nowadays, but the gracious villas and elegant palm-lined promenades which characterise many of the resorts and spots such as Lerici, Rapallo and Portofino are as prestigious as they ever were. The attraction of the region also lies in its all-year-round temperate climate, and the shelter from the cold east winds provided by the mountains.

The architecture along the coast, as well as being typified by turn-of-the-century villas, has many *palazzi* with monochrome painted façades and sometimes *trompe l'oeil* decorations. The architecture inland and away from the resorts and cities is quite different, with small stone hamlets in the hinterland and fishing villages along the coast, the most spectacular of which are those in the Cinque Terre, one of the steepest and most dramatic coastlands in Italy.

Due to the steepness of the terrain, agriculture is limited. The hills are stacked into almost vertical terraces of olives and vines in places. Liguria is also known for its flower-growing, particularly carnations, which unfortunately means that unsightly greenhouses often mar the view. First and foremost, however, the Ligurian economy is based on industry. Genoa has the largest industrial zone in Italy as well as a very important port. Savona and La Spezia also have large commercial ports and their own fair share of industry.

The Ligurians are not short of money, although they are sometimes seen by other Italians as the 'most careful' people in the nation. Property is expensively priced, particularly along the coast where the value of property has soared due to strict building regulations. In Genoa, the property market was also on the upturn until 1992. Since then it has, however, experienced a decline. 1992 closed with a sharp fall in buyers. 1993 prices are down 11.8 per cent for property in the suburbs, 20 per cent

Property prices		
Location	Condition	Price
Genoa	New	2.5–3.0
	Recent	2.5
	Old	1.5–3.5
La Spezia	New	2.5–3.0
Coast	Detached	2.5–10.0
	Resort	2.0–7.0
	Periphery	1.5–5.0
Land prices		
Province	Type	Price
Genoa	Cultivated	1.5–25.0
	Uncultivated	1.5–2.5
	Meadow	7.0–10.0
	Forest	4.0–8.0
Imperia	Cultivated	5.5–20.5
	Uncultivated	0.5–1.5
	Meadow	4.5–11.0
	Forest	4.0–5.0
La Spezia	Cultivated	5.0–25.5
	Uncultivated	1.0–2.0
	Meadow	4.0–8.0
	Forest	1.0–2.0
Savona	Cultivated	8.0–21.0
	Uncultivated	0.5–1.5
	Meadow	4.0–5.0
	Forest	2.5–5.0

Fig. 9. Property and land prices in Liguria.

29

outer city areas and 13 per cent in the historic centre. The outlook a period of stability, although it is feared that the number of buyers / continue to drop.

For an idea of property and land prices in Liguria see Fig. 9 (page 29).

Lombardy

Area	23,834 km^2
Population	8,891,318
Inhabitants per km^2	371
Regional capital	Milan
Provincial capitals	Bergamo, Brescia, Como, Cremona, Mantova, Milan, Pavia, Sondrio, Varese
Airports	Milan, Bergamo

The region of Lombardy has a diverse landscape which ranges from the flat alluvial plain of the Po river to the gently rolling hills that gradually rise to the dramatic peaks of the Alps which shelter Italy's famous northern lakes. Lombardy is also crammed full of art and architecture, stylish shops and high-quality restaurants. It is the richest region in Italy and also the most expensive. Most Lombards would prefer to have nothing to do with the rest of Italy, feeling that it only hinders them.

Wealth is gained not only from industry, which is mainly concentrated around Milan, Brescia, Pavia and Varese, but also from agriculture. The soils of the Po valley are rich and well-watered and yield a wide range of high-density and quality crops through the use of modern farming methods. One of the negative aspects of the region is its climate. Although the northern lakes and the Alps enjoy a dry climate, elsewhere it is very often damp and foggy. Winter arrives early and summer is stiflingly hot and humid.

To uplift the spirits in times of gloomy weather the Lombards drink *grappa* (spirit) often flavoured with myrtle. The further north you travel in Lombardy you will also find other additions to the diet such as German beer, black sausages and wurstel, while *polenta* (maize flour) is one of the basic staple foods throughout Lombardy.

Property in Lombardy, like everything else, is very expensive, exclusively so around the northern lakes where luxurious villas are set in luscious gardens. Property in the capital Milan is also fairly prohibitively priced. 1991 saw a 25.8 per cent increase in sales, although this doesn't amount to much when taking into account the decrease in 1992 of 21.9 per cent. The current trend is for prices, particularly of properties in the suburbs, to creep upwards. The provincial capitals of Lombardy share this trend with the exception of property in Bergamo, Varese and Como where

	Property prices	
Location	*Condition*	*Price*
Milan	New	2.5–7.5
	Recent	3.3–8.0
	Old	2.5–6.0
Bergamo	New	1.4–1.6
Brescia	New	2.2–3.7
Como	New	1.6–2.3
Cremona	New	2.0–2.3
Mantua	New	1.7–2.6
Pavia	New	1.9–3.1
Varese	New	1.7–2.3
Mountains	Detached	3.0–6.5
	Resort	2.5–5.0
	Periphery	1.5–3.9
	Land prices	
Province	*Type*	*Price*
Bergamo	Cultivated	25.0–32.5
	Uncultivated	3.5–5.0
	Meadow	24.0–33.5
	Forest	12.5
Brescia	Cultivated	12.5–24.0
	Uncultivated	1.0–2.0
	Meadow	11.0–18.0
	Forest	5.5–12.0
Como	Cultivated	18.0–26.0
	Uncultivated	1.0–5.0
	Meadow	16.0–23.5
	Forest	1.5–6.5

Fig. 10. Property and land prices in Lombardy.

| | Land prices continued | |
Province	Type	Price
Cremona	Cultivated	18.0–40.0
	Uncultivated	4.0–5.5
	Meadow	13.0–16.5
	Forest	—
Mantua	Cultivated	26.0–36.5
	Uncultivated	6.5–7.0
	Meadow	14.5–17.5
	Forest	26.0–33.0
Milan	Cultivated	26.5–31.0
	Uncultivated	13.0–16.5
	Meadow	26.5–31.0
	Forest	11.5–14.5
Pavia	Cultivated	8.0–32.0
	Uncultivated	2.0–3.5
	Meadow	8.0–23.5
	Forest	3.0–18.0
Sondrio	Cultivated	15.5–20.0
	Uncultivated	1.0–1.5
	Meadow	23.0–27.0
	Forest	3.5–4.5
Varese	Cultivated	14.5–28.0
	Uncultivated	3.0–5.5
	Meadow	12.0–22.5
	Forest	5.0–9.0

Fig. 10. Continued

the top end of the market is on a decline. For an idea of property and land prices in Lombardy, see Fig. 10 (pages 31-32).

Marches

Area	9,694 km^2
Population	1,420,829
Inhabitants per km^2	146
Regional capital	Ancona
Provincial capitals	Ancona, Ascoli Piceno, Macerata, Pesaro, Urbino
Airports	Ancona, Rimini

The Marches is one of the most under-rated regions in Italy. It is characterised by a splendid landscape, mostly hilly or mountainous, which is dotted with charming hill towns and villages, many of which are reminiscent of Tuscany. The Marches also enjoys a long stretch of the Adriatic coast which is edged by flat sandy beaches all the way, with the exception of the Conero, a headland that rises to a height of 572 m.

Unfortunately, there is a railway and a motorway to contend with as well as some hideous coastal developments. Excellent fish restaurants partly compensate and there are some delightful coves and places to reach by boat off the Conero. The Conero is also a centre of red wine-making, while excellent white wine, Verdicchio, is made around Jesi and Matelica.

The local economy has improved greatly over the last decade with the development of new industries and the use of modern farming techniques to cultivate cereals and grains, as well as fruit along the coast. Some of the traditional industries of the region are shoe-making at Civitanova, paper-making at Fabriano and majolica ceramic making at Pesaro and Urbino. Other main centres of industry are Ancona, Pesaro and Falconara Marittima where there is a large petrochemical works.

The local architecture is typified by gracious *palazzi* in the towns built of small bricks, while stone farms and farm-workers' houses dot the countryside. The numerous villages also have some surprisingly dignified architecture as well as picturesque narrow streets. The property market in the Marches is still relatively behind the times and it is possible to find very cheap properties that are in need of renovation. Often, however, such properties are virtually inaccessible, without roads or any services.

Property in towns and on the coast, with the exception of Pesaro, has suffered from the general decline in the property market and the maximum prices for 1993 were considerably lower than those for 1992. A guide to prices in the Marches is given in Fig. 11 (page 34).

	Property prices	
Location	Condition	Price
Ancona	New	1.6–2.4
Ascoli Piceno	New	1.2–1.4
Pesaro	New	2.0–2.6
Coast	Detached	1.5–3.5
	Resort	1.3–2.8
	Periphery	1.3–2.5
	Land prices	
Province	Type	Price
Ancona	Cultivated	8.5–18.0
	Uncultivated	2.5–3.0
	Meadow	6.0–10.5
	Forest	5.0–7.0
Ascoli Piceno	Cultivated	4.0–13.0
	Uncultivated	1.5–2.0
	Meadow	3.5–5.0
	Forest	3.0–7.5
Macerata	Cultivated	8.0–20.0
	Uncultivated	2.0–2.5
	Meadow	4.5–5.5
	Forest	4.0–6.0
Pesaro	Cultivated	7.5–18.5
	Uncultivated	2.0–2.5
	Meadow	2.5–6.0
	Forest	3.5–6.0

Fig. 11. Property and land prices in the Marches.

Molise

Area	4,438 km^2
Population	331,670
Inhabitants per km^2	75
Regional capital	Campobasso
Provincial capitals	Campobasso, Isernia
Airports	Pescara, Naples, Foggia

The region of Molise is where north and south Italy meet. There is the orderliness of the north but also the poverty of the south. The region is more fertile and better-watered than regions further south, having a well-forested landscape and many wide river valleys which are intensely cultivated with grains, cereals and potatoes. Areas of coastal plain bordering the Adriatic are also cultivated. Most of the terrain, however, is too steep for farming. The Matese mountains, which belong to the Apennine chain, are the highest point of the region with peaks reaching up to 2,050m. The mountains are used for sheep-rearing which, other than agriculture, is the main form of income in the region.

Industry has not really developed very much, except around Termoli. Traditional cottage industries include knife-making at Campobasso and Frosonone, and also bell-founding at Agnone. The poor economy of the region is not helped by the frequent occurrence of earthquakes which have devastated many towns. Isernia, the capital of the province, still bears the scars of the earthquake of 1984 and even now whole sections of the town are propped up by stout wooden scaffolding.

Property in Molise is not rated very highly and the region is not popular either as a holiday destination or as a place to live. For an idea of property and land prices in Molise see Fig. 12 (page 36).

Piedmont

Area	25,399 km^2
Population	4,431,064
Inhabitants per km^2	174
Regional capital	Turin
Provincial capitals	Alessandria, Asti, Cuneo, Novara, Turin, Vercelli
Airports	Turin, Malpensa

Piedmont shares the northern character of neighbouring Lombardy, but the region is generally less expensive and has better wines and food. Like

Property prices

Location	Condition	Price
Campobasso	New	1.1–2.5
	Recent	1.1–2.5
	Old	0.7–2.3

Land prices

Province	Type	Price
Campobasso	Cultivated	7.0–23.0
	Uncultivated	1.0–4.5
	Meadow	7.0–13.0
	Forest	5.0–9.5
Isernia	Cultivated	6.0–17.5
	Uncultivated	1.5–3.0
	Meadow	7.0–9.5
	Forest	5.0–9.0

Fig. 12. Property and land prices in Molise.

	Property prices	
Location	*Condition*	*Price*
Turin	New	3.5–6.5
	Recent	1.7–4.5
	Old	0.8–3.5
Alessandria	New	1.4–2.0
Cuneo	New	1.4–1.9
Novara	New	1.4–2.2
Vercelli	New	1.3–1.8
Mountains	Detached	3.0–6.0
	Resort	3.0–5.0
	Periphery	2.0–4.0
	Land prices	
Province	*Type*	*Price*
Alessandria	Cultivated	7.5–17.0
	Pasture	1.0–2.5
	Forest	5.5–17.6
Asti	Cultivated	8.0–16.0
	Pasture	1.0–1.2
	Forest	8.0–10.0
Cuneo	Cultivated	3.5–21.0
	Pasture	1.0–4.0
	Forest	10.0–30.0
Novara	Cultivated	11.0.–20.0
	Pasture	3.0–6.0
	Forest	3.0–10.0
Turin	Cultivated	16.0–35.0
	Pasture	1.7–4.2
	Forest	7.0–10.0
Vercelli	Cultivated	5.5–13.5
	Pasture	1.0–4.0
	Forest	4.5–10.5

Fig. 13. Property and land prices in Piedmont.

Lombardy, Piedmont is over-towered by the Alps, although it has fewer lakes, and has vast flat plains surrounding the Po. Piedmont also has a delightful region of hills, south of the Po, known as the Langhe. Asti Spumante and Cinzano originated from here as do some of Italy's most prestigious red wines. The Langhe boasts a number of charming wine-making châteaux and is an area that is particularly popular with British and Dutch holiday-makers.

Agriculture in Piedmont is wide-ranging although one of the more important crops is rice. Piedmont's industry, centred on Turin, is largely based on car manufacturing with Fiat leading the way. More traditional Piedmont industries include the production of wool. In the vicinity of Biella, old and often abandoned wool mills line the river valleys. Textiles, particularly artificial fibre, continue to be important and it is here that much of the clothing for Italy's fashion industry is produced.

The architecture in Piedmont is as varied as the landscape. In the mountainous regions there are many small hamlets where the houses are built of grey stone and have either slate or stone-tiled roofs. In the flatter fertile regions there are elegant villas dating from the eighteenth and nineteenth centuries with red roofs and surrounding parklands. Due to the wealth of the region there is also a considerable amount of modern architecture which is both well-built and professionally designed.

The property market is varied. Properties in the more remote regions of the Langhe are reasonably priced while a flat in Turin will fetch an exorbitant sum. The 1980s saw a boom in property in Turin. Since 1992, however, the market has settled somewhat with a slight drop in the number of buyers and stability in the prices for property on the city outskirts. City centre and suburban properties continue to gain value with prices up by 10 per cent in 1992. The outlook for the property market in Turin is stable. Some general prices for land and property in Piedmont are given in Fig. 13 (p. 37).

Puglia

Area	19,347 km^2
Population	3,946,871
Inhabitants per km^2	204
Regional capital	Bari
Provincial capitals	Bari, Brindisi, Foggia, Lecce, Taranto
Airports	Bari, Brindisi, Foggia

The region of Puglia is relatively flat apart from a range of gently undulating hills, the Murge, along the Ionian coast and a splendid rocky peninsula, the Gargano, which juts out into the Adriatic. Although the

Property prices

Location	Condition	Price
Bari	New	2.5–6.5
	Old	1.8–2.5
Brindisi	New	0.9–1.1
Foggia	New	1.6–2.2
Lecce	New	1.4–2.0
Taranto	New	1.8–2.2
Coast	Detached	1.5–3.5
	Resort	1.1–2.5
	Periphery	0.7–3.0

Land prices

Province	Type	Price
Brindisi	Cultivated	6.5–9.0
	Meadow	2.0
	Forest	3.0–5.5
Foggia	Cultivated	6.0–12.0
	Meadow	2.0–4.5
	Forest	3.0–4.5
Lecce	Cultivated	6.0–11.5
	Meadow	2.0–3.5
	Forest	6.0–7.0
Taranto	Cultivated	6.0–8.5
	Meadow	2.0–3.5
	Forest	3.5–4.5
Bari	Cultivated	5.0–8.0
	Meadow	2.0–2.5
	Forest	3.0–3.5

Fig. 14. Property and land prices in Puglia.

coast is not mountainous only 34 per cent is made up of sandy beaches, most of which are to be found along the Adriatic. The coastline is otherwise rocky with low red cliffs along the Ionian.

Despite a chronic shortage of water with only two major rivers and a very low annual rainfall, the Puglian economy is largely dependent on agriculture. The land is covered by mile after mile of olive groves, many containing a giant variety of the olive tree, and endless vineyards. The vines on the Salentine peninsula, the heel of Italy's boot, are particularly noted both as table grapes and for wine. In the north of the region, the great plain known as the Tavoliere around Foggia produces 3/5 of Italy's durum wheat, the essential ingredient of pasta.

Puglia also has a fair amount of industry. At Taranto there is an iron and steel works, at Barletta cement manufacturers and at Brindisi a petrochemicals plant. Taranto and Brindisi are also important ports, the latter being the main point of embarkation for Greece. The cities of Puglia rate with the roughest and toughest in Italy. Crime is commonplace and the threat of the Mafia is ever-present. With the exception of Lecce, which has some outstanding Baroque architecture, the cities of Puglia are probably best avoided.

By contrast, the countryside and the property in it are very attractive. Rural Puglia is reminiscent of southern Greece, being littered with neatly whitewashed, little cube-shaped houses that are draped with bougainvillaea and other flowering climbers. Puglia is also the region of *trulli* houses, unusual cone-shaped dwellings built of stone, and now a major tourist attraction. It has become quite fashionable to buy a *trulli* and restore it as a holiday home.

The price of property in Puglia is fairly reasonable. In Bari, the capital of the region, property has dropped in value over the last year and there has been a decrease in the number of buyers. Sales were down by 14.8 per cent in 1992 and are probably going to continue to fall in the foreseeable future. The only property that has maintained its value is that in the historic centre on the city outskirts. A guide to the prices of land and property in Puglia can be seen in Fig. 14 (page 39).

Sardinia

Area	24,089 km^2
Population	1,617,265
Inhabitants per km^2	67
Regional capital	Cagliari
Provincial capitals	Cagliari, Nuoro, Oristano, Sassari
Airports	Alghero, Cagliari, Olbia

Sardinia, the second largest island in the Mediterranean, is the most sparsely populated region of Italy. The landscape is harsh, the soils barren and the coasts are either rocky or marshy. There are some 400,000 hectares of woods, among which are extensive forests of cork trees which provide an exciting splash of colour. The Campidano, a vast plain between Cagliari and Oristano, provides at least some fertile land. Agriculture elsewhere on the island is restricted to the cultivation of vines and olives.

The south-west used to be a centre of mining, but the industry has virtually ground to a halt now, leaving mineheads and slag heaps to scar the land. New industries in Sardinia include petrochemicals at Cagliari and Porto Torres; the latter also has a large plastics industry.

Otherwise the economy is based on sheep rearing. Sardinian *pecorino* (sheep's cheese) is among the best in Italy, while the sheep's wool is used in the weaving of textiles for tourism. Tourism is one of Sardinia's more prosperous industries. It is becoming an increasingly popular destination with Italians for the August holiday as even in peak season quiet beaches and clean seas can still be found.

It was the Ahga Khan who first introduced tourism to the island in the 1960s when he bought up a stretch of coast, now known as the Costa Smeralda. The resorts and villages developed here are for millionaires only and life here is a shocking contrast to the rest of the island. New holiday homes built elsewhere along the coast often try to copy the Costa Smeralda look which, apart from being expensive, is meant to appear 'hand-made'. Building specifications often include top-quality terracotta, travertine, handmade ceramic tiles and chestnut beams. Elsewhere on the island the architecture is very simple with stone shepherd's crofts in the mountains and simple fisherman's houses on the coast. Town architecture tends to be rather dour and unlike other Italian towns few have piazzas.

Most people who visit Sardinia, including D.H. Lawrence, have come to the conclusion that it is a place for holidays rather than long-term stays. The wet, cold winters and the lack of employment prospects are negative factors in settling down here. This is reflected in the decline in the property market of the capital, Cagliari. Both sales and prices have fallen steadily since 1991. Properties in the historic centre have been downgraded and the trend for the future is one of a continuing fall. Cagliari's rival city, Sassari, on the other hand is prospering and property prices in 1993 were considerably higher than those in 1992.

Property on the coast is also better rated, particularly around the resorts. The Costa Smeraldo is beyond most budgets; Alghero, the other principal and only long-established resort on the island is also pricy. Alghero, however, is a place that most people, particularly the British, fly to on a

	Property prices	
Location	Condition	Price
Cagliari	New	2.1–3.2
	Recent	1.6–2.0
	Old	1.5–1.7
Nuoro	New	1.1–1.4
Oristano	New	1.0–1.3
Sassari	New	1.5–1.8
Coast	Detached	3.5–9.0
	Resort	3.0–8.0
	Periphery	2.5–6.0
	Land prices	
Province	Type	Price
Cagliari	Cultivated	5.0–16.0
	Uncultivated	1.0–2.5
	Meadow	2.5–5.0
	Forest	4.5–7.5
Oristano	Cultivated	5.0–12.0
	Uncultivated	1.1–2.5
	Meadow	3.0–4.0
	Forest	4.5–5.0
Nuoro	Cultivated	4.0–8.0
	Uncultivated	1.5–2.0
	Meadow	3.5–5.5
	Forest	3.5–5.0
Sassari	Cultivated	5.0–8.5
	Uncultivated	1.5–2.5
	Meadow	3.5–6.5
	Forest	4.0–5.0

Fig. 15. Property and land prices in Sardinia.

package holiday. For an idea of prices of land and property in Sardinia see Fig. 15 (page 42).

Sicily

Area	25,708 km2
Population	5,006,684
Inhabitants per km2	195
Regional capital	Palermo
Provincial capitals	Agrigento, Caltanissetta, Catania, Enna, Messina, Palermo, Ragusa, Syracuse, Trapani
Airports	Palermo, Catania, Trapani

Sicily, the largest and most densely populated island in the Mediterranean is no longer a holiday-maker's paradise. The coast is littered with shabby resorts and industry. Added to this, nearly all the towns and cities have slum-like outskirts, the worst of which are at Palermo and Catania. The attractions of Sicily lie in its grime and disorder which often conceal a wealth of art treasures and ancient sites.

Up until the last decade, Sicily was dependent on agriculture, a role that it has played since ancient Roman times, particularly for the production of grain. It is still the major producer in Italy of durum wheat, but industry has reared into the foreground with unsightly petrol refineries, chemical and plastics factories, and cement works on the coast at Augusta-Siracusa, Gela, Porto Empedocle and Milazzo. Palermo and Catania are also major industrial centres.

The countryside, despite being parched most of the year round, is surprisingly green with eucalyptus, citrus and olive trees in abundance. Prickly pear cactus and vines are also profuse. The landscape is mostly hilly with eroded gullies, ridges and wide open views being typical features.

Architecture in Sicily is flavoured with a touch of Arabic, many of the smaller towns comprising cube-shaped houses with flat roofs. In the hilly regions houses are stacked higgledy-piggledy and most towns and villages have a weather-beaten Baroque church. Modern developments have a similar sense of disorder, but without the charm. Many modern buildings lie unfinished and most are flimsily built.

Property in Sicily is undesirable mainly due to the Mafia problems. Property in Palermo, the reputed Mafia headquarters, fell into a decline in 1991 losing 12 per cent in the number of sales. However, Palermo has led the way in recent months to an open protest against Mafia control and

	Property prices	
Location	*Condition*	*Price*
Palermo	New	1.6–3.6
	Recent	1.3–3.1
	Old	0.9–2.6
Agrigento	New	1.6–2.0
Catania	New	1.6–2.0
Messina	New	2.0–3.5
Syracuse	New	1.4–1.6
Trapani	New	1.0–1.5
Coast	Detached	2.0–3.0
	Resort	1.0–3.0
	Periphery	0.8–2.5
	Land prices	
Province	*Type*	*Price*
Agrigento	Cultivated	4.5–8.5
	Meadow	2.0–3.0
	Forest	3.0–4.0
Caltanissetta	Cultivated	6.0–7.0
	Meadow	2.0–2.5
	Forest	4.0–4.5

Fig. 16. Property and land prices in Sicily.

Land prices continued		
Province	*Type*	*Price*
Catania	Cultivated	6.0–9.0
	Meadow	3.5–4.5
	Forest	4.5–6.5
Enna	Cultivated	8.0–10.5
	Meadow	3.0–4.0
	Forest	5.0–6.5
Messina	Cultivated	3.0–11.5
	Meadow	2.0–2.5
	Forest	2.0–2.5
Palermo	Cultivated	6.5–9.5
	Meadow	2.0–3.5
	Forest	2.0–3.0
Ragusa	Cultivated	5.5–7.5
	Meadow	3.5
Syracuse	Cultivated	5.0–8.0
	Meadow	2.0–3.0
	Forest	2.0–2.5
Trapani	Cultivated	5.0–9.5
	Meadow	2.0–3.0
	Forest	3.0

Fig. 16. Continued.

sales have since gradually increased. Prices have also been gradually climbing up with an outlook for a period of stability in the future and a steady increase in the value of city centre properties. Fig. 16 outlines some of the general prices for property and land both in Palermo and other areas of Sicily (pages 44-45).

Trentino-Alto Adige

Area	6,213 km^2
Population	13,613
Inhabitants per km^2	122
Regional capitals	Bolzano, Trento
Airports	Milan, Venice, Verona

Trentino-Alto Adige is made up of two autonomous provinces: Trentino, the capital of which is Trento, and Alto Adige whose capital is Bolzano. The region as a whole has been granted semi-autonomy since 1948. The Alto Adige region is dominated by the Alps which divide Italy from Austria. Until 1918 the region was part of the Austro-Hungarian Empire. German is widely spoken and there is still a good deal of Austrian influence both in the local food and architecture.

Decorative towers, multi-coloured slates, very steeply pitched roofs and Baroque cupolas are just some features of the local town architecture. In the mountains local architecture is typified by the small chalets known as *baite*, and their larger counterparts, which are built of wood and white-painted stone, with overhanging slate roofs and dark-wood balconies. In the more gentle hilly areas there are numerous fine estates and many *castelli* (castles), with neat red roofs and turrets.

The region is best known for its skiing facilities which are among the most modern in Italy. The economy, however, is also based on a certain amount of agriculture with dairy farming and fruit growing (apples and pears) being very common.

The province of Trentino is also very mountainous but contains many rivers and valleys including that of the Adige. Agriculture is similar to that of Alto Adige, while the dense forests also provide raw material for industries that use wood. Like Alto Adige, however, tourism is of prime importance.

There is a lot of property for holiday-makers in the region of Trentino-Alto Adige. Therefore settling down in the region means contending with the holiday resort atmosphere. You can be fairly sure, however, of making a good investment and buying a well-built and designed property. For an idea of prices see Fig. 17 (page 47).

Property prices

Location	Condition	Price
Bolzano	New	5.0
	Recent	4.0
	Old	3.5
Trento	New	1.8–2.5
Mountains	Detached	2.6–8.0
	Resort	2.0–8.5
	Periphery	1.8–4.7

Land prices

Province	Type	Price
Bolzano	Cultivated	6.0–15.0
	Uncultivated	1.0–5.0
	Meadow	5.5–7.5
	Forest	1.0–1.5
Trento	Cultivated	35.0–75.0
	Uncultivated	6.0–26.0
	Meadow	26.0–53.0
	Forest	4.5–6.5

Fig. 17. Property and land prices in Trentino-Alto Adige.

Tuscany

Area	22,992 km^2
Population	3,581,291
Inhabitants per km^2	156
Regional capital	Florence
Provincial capitals	Arezzo, Grosseto, Florence, Livorno, Lucca, Massa-Carrara, Pisa, Pistoia, Siena
Airports	Florence, Pisa, Rome

Central Tuscany with its hill towns, art treasures, vineyards and cypress trees is a delightful area. Other areas of Tuscany are quite diverse. The wide and fertile valley of the Arno river, which flows through Florence and Pisa before emptying into the Tyrrhenian coast, is intensely cultivated with market gardens and flower-growing. The north of the region has the Apennines, the foothills of which, known as the Garfagnana, are thickly wooded.

The Tuscan coast is also varied. The northern part is backed by the jagged peaks of the Apuan Alps which are quarried for marble. The south, by contrast is completely flat with lagoons, marshes and sandy beaches backed by pine forests.

Tuscan architecture is typified by the stone farmhouse set on a hill with a token cypress tree, olive orchard and vineyard. The stone of the region is warm-coloured as are the rich terracotta roofs. To add to the general glow there are many fine villas and *palazzi* painted in traditional Tuscan red. On a less grand scale, but nonetheless attractive, are the farmworkers' houses dotted around the countryside and the lovely stone-built towns, where the windows and doors are often arched and where the *palazzi* are interspersed with numerous medieval towers.

Property in central Tuscany, along with that around the northern lakes, is the most expensive in Italy. The British have swarmed to this area in their hoards, buying up barns for conversion when failing to procure the classic Tuscan farmhouse. British housing agents deal with the British market as much as possible, although you will pay above the odds for this privilege.

The most expensive properties are those that are within a 30 km radius of Florence, Siena or Pisa. In Florence itself sales were up to 85.5 per cent in 1991 and prices have increased by up to 30 per cent since. Old properties, which are the most in demand, are expected to continue increasing in value. If you are determined to have a Tuscan farmhouse but

	Property prices	
Location	*Condition*	*Price*
Florence	New	2.5–6.0
	Recent	2.0–3.8
	Old	1.7–3.0
Arezzo	New	2.7–2.3
Grosseto	New	1.4–1.7
Livorno	New	2.1–2.7
Pisa	New	2.2–2.5
Siena	New	3.0–5.0
Coast	Detached	2.6–10.0
	Resort	2.0–10.0
	Periphery	1.7–8.0
Mountains	Resort	1.3–3.5
	Periphery	1.0–3.0
	Land prices	
Province	*Type*	*Price*
Arezzo	Cultivated	3.5–15.0
	Uncultivated	1.0–2.0
	Meadow	3.0–4.0
	Forest	4.5–5.5
Florence	Cultivated	3.5–18.0
	Uncultivated	1.0–2.5
	Meadow	3.0–4.0
	Forest	4.5–5.5

Fig. 18. Property and land prices in Tuscany.

Land prices continued		
Province	*Type*	*Price*
Grosseto	Cultivated	3.0–13.0
	Uncultivated	1.0–2.0
	Meadow	4.5–9.0
	Forest	3.5–11.00
Livorno	Cultivated	11.0–14.0
	Uncultivated	2.5–3.0
	Meadow	5.5–6.5
	Forest	5.5–7.5
Massa-Carrara	Cultivated	9.0–26.0
	Uncultivated	3.0–3.5
	Meadow	8.0–25.5
	Forest	8.5–10.5
Pisa	Cultivated	5.5–13.5
	Uncultivated	2.0–2.5
	Meadow	4.0–6.0
	Forest	4.0–6.0
Pistoia	Cultivated	4.0–23.0
	Uncultivated	1.5
	Meadow	5.0–11.0
	Forest	5.0–11.0
Siena	Cultivated	7.0–14.5
	Uncultivated	1.5–2.0
	Meadow	4.0–6.0
	Forest	4.0–6.0

Fig. 18. Continued.

have a limited budget, areas further afield such as to the north of Lucca and around Arezzo may be worth considering.

Areas to avoid in Tuscany are those built up with industry, namely the industrial belt that stretches along the Arno from Florence to Prato, Pistoia and Lucca. There is also some unsightly industrial development on the coast at Livorno where there is a petrol refinery and at Orbetello where minerals are extracted. Properties on the coast are mostly holiday homes; settling here all year round involves sitting out a cold windswept winter when the resorts are completely dead.

See Fig. 18 for the going rates for land and property in Tuscany.

Umbria

Area	8,456 km^2
Population	813,507
Inhabitants per km^2	96
Regional capital	Perugia
Provincial capitals	Perugia, Terni
Airports	Perugia, Ancona, Rome

Situated in the very centre of the country, Umbria is known by the tourist brochures as the green heart of Italy. It is a generally mountainous and somewhat inaccessible region containing the Central Apennines, although there are no peaks higher than 1,500 m, and the landscape is made up of gentle hills. The undeniable greenness of Umbria is partly because the region is yet to be ravaged by man and partly because it is well-watered by natural sources, rivers and lakes, among the most popular of which is Lake Trasimeno.

Among the hills there are several large flat basins, such as those around Gubbio, Terni and Nocera, and also wide river valleys, the largest of which carries the Tiber between Perugia and Spoleto. These flat areas are cultivated with grain, while the surrounding hills are covered in olive groves and vineyards. Industry, which is fast eating into the flatter areas of the region, is concentrated around Terni, Foligno, Perugia and Narni.

Umbrian architecture is sombre but attractive. The stone is lighter in colour than that of Tuscany but the building style is quite similar with hilltop villages and farming hamlets scattering the landscape and arches being widely used for windows and doors.

Small and narrow archways set into the walls of houses in Umbria are

Property prices

Location	Condition	Price
Perugia	New	1.2–1.7
Terni	New	1.4–1.7

Land prices

Province	Type	Price
Perugia	Cultivated	4.0–12.0
	Uncultivated	1.0–3.5
	Pasture	1.5–3.5
	Forest	2.5–5.0
Terni	Cultivated	4.5–10.0
	Uncultivated	1.0–2.0
	Pasture	1.6–3.5
	Forest	2.5–5.0

Fig. 19. Property and land prices in Umbria.

known as *Porte della Morte* (doors of death). Whether it is true or not it is said that when there was a death in the house the coffin would be carried out through this opening. Most are bricked up now. Towers are another typical feature: fat, thin, tall and short, sometimes converted into independent living accommodation and sometimes incorporated into a house. You will also notice fine wrought-iron work throughout the region, in the form of balconies, lamp posts, grills on windows and other architectural features.

The similarities with Tuscany mean that property in Umbria is being brought to the attention of the British buying public as an alternative. In Italy the region is generally cast off as a backwater due to the lack of employment prospects. However, local holiday-makers go to Lake Trasimeno, while the Umbrian countryside is gaining popularity with the Romans as a weekend retreat being within striking distance of Rome. For an idea of the price of land and property in Umbria see Fig. 19 (page 52).

Valle d'Aosta

Area	3,262 km^2
Population	113,418
Inhabitants per km^2	35
Regional capital	Aosta
Provincial capitals	Aosta
Airports	Milan, Turin

The semi-autonomous region of Valle d'Aosta is officially bi-lingual, with French and Italian both spoken. The region butts up to the highest of the Alpine peaks that run along the French and Swiss border, including Mont Blanc (4,810 m), the Matterhorn (4,478 m) and Monte Rosa (4,633 m). It also contains the dramatic peak of Monte Paradiso (4,061 m) which is surrounded by a national park.

The region is well-endowed with resorts both for summer and winter recreation, the best known of which is Courmayeur. Typical houses of the region are known as *rascards* (chalets built of wood and uncut stone). Properties such as these fetch high prices but are very sturdily built and well-designed. Property in general is more expensive than in equivalent resorts in neighbouring Piedmont and it is said that the people are somewhat reserved.

Some general prices for land and property are given in Fig. 20 (p. 54).

Property prices

Location	Condition	Price
Aosta	New	2.5–6.5
	Old	1.8–2.5
Mountains	Detached	2.6–7.0
	Resort	2.0–8.5
	Periphery	1.8–7.0

Land prices

Province	Type	Price
Aosta	Cultivated	5.0–7.5
	Uncultivated	0.5–1.0
	Meadow	6.0–12.0
	Forest	2.5–3.5

Fig. 20. Property and land prices in Valle d'Aosta.

Veneto

Area	18,377 km^2
Population	4,361,527
Inhabitants per km^2	237
Regional capital	Venice
Provincial capitals	Belluno, Padua, Rovigo, Treviso, Venice, Verona, Vicenza
Airports	Verona, Venice

The region of Veneto has the eastern Alps in the north and a vast alluvial plain in the south. The plain is formed by numerous rivers, including the Po, that empty into the Adriatic. It is intensely cultivated with cereals and potatoes. Other agricultural products of the region include fruit (pear, apple, peach and cherry), dairy products and grapes which are grown on the foothills of the Alps. It is also among the highest producers in Italy of sugar beet and tobacco.

The jewel of Veneto is the beautiful city of Venice. However, there are many other fine towns with distinctive Venetian architecture typified by slender arched windows, balconies and elegant loggias. Many buildings are built of Verona stone which is a warm pink colour, while others are painted with pastel-coloured façades and contrastingly dark wooden shutters. The countryside too is well-endowed with Venetian architecture, including stately homes and villas.

Venice is said to be the most expensive city in Italy. Property is certainly beyond the average budget. However, it is possible to find rural properties within an hour's drive of Venice at more reasonable prices. A guide to prices for property and land is given in Fig. 21 (pages 56-57).

Location	Condition	Price
Property prices		
Venice	New	4.0–8.0
	Recent	3.5–5.0
	Old	2.5–4.0
Rovigo	New	1.2–1.6
Treviso	New	2.1–3.1
Verona	New	1.7–2.1
Vicenza	New	1.3–2.1
Coast	Detached	1.3–5.0
	Resort	1.2–5.0
	Periphery	1.0–3.5
Mountains	Detached	2.5–18.0
	Resort	2.4–18.0
	Periphery	1.5–13.0

Fig. 21. Property and land prices in Veneto.

Land prices

Province	Type	Price
Belluno	Cultivated	30.0–34.0
	Meadow	20.0–22.5
	Forest	10.0–12.0
Padua	Cultivated	39.0–45.0
	Meadow	28.0–37.0
	Forest	10.0–14.0
Rovigo	Cultivated	29.0–30.5
Treviso	Cultivated	32.0–40.0
	Meadow	22.0–29.0
	Forest	10.0–14.0
Vicenza	Cultivated	25.0–40.0
	Meadow	29.0–47.0
	Forest	15.0–20.0
Venice	Cultivated	28.5–31.0
	Meadow	22.0–25.0
	Forest	15.0–16.5
Verona	Cultivated	28.5–41.0
	Meadow	27.5–40.0
	Forest	13.0–15.0

Fig. 21. Continued.

2
Renting

TYPES OF ACCOMMODATION

Holiday lets

Holiday flats and villas, either on the coast or in mountain resorts, are by far the most readily available type of rented accommodation as many Italians have second homes which sit empty for most of the year in these places.

As well as the normal holiday lets there is also a system known as **Agriturismo**. Agriturismo is an organisation that rents out rooms in family homes in rural locations. The great majority of Agriturismo accommodation is concentrated in Trentino-Alto Adige, Tuscany and Umbria, and more recently in Sardinia. The accommodation varies, ranging from the basic bed and breakfast where you may be expected to offer some work in exchange, to the country hotel which will probably have a tennis court and pool. Most Agriturismo lodgings are affiliated to a regional organisation which determines the tariffs. To find out more about Agriturismo holidays request the *Guida dell'Ospitalita Rurale* from the address below:

Agriturist
Corso Vittorio Emanuele 101
Rome
Tel: (06) 6512342.

Alternatively, contact the following regional organisations:

Terra Nostra
Via XXIV Maggio 43
Rome
Tel: (06) 4682368.

Turismo Verde
Via Mariano Fortuny 20
Rome
Tel: (06) 3969931.

Associazione Agriturismo Trentino
Via Rosmini 42
Trento
Tel: (0461) 36211.

Sudtiroler Bauernbund
Perathonerstrasse 10
Bolzano
Tel: (0471) 27145.

Cooperative Allevatrici Sarde
Casella Postale 107
Oristano (Sardinia)
Tel: (0783) 4818066.

Long-term lets

In towns or cities the selection of rented accommodation is limited mainly to apartments of varying sizes, as they suit the style of living that the majority of Italian families prefer. Most cities have a lot of rented accommodation as it is quite common for families to make long-term rentals rather than buy their own property. Consequently the demand for rented property often exceeds the supply and it can be difficult to find available apartments, especially those that are on the market at a reasonable price.

The vast majority of apartments for rent belong to a condominium, an apartment block which shares facilities such as lifts, boilers, cleaning services and air-conditioning. General information regarding life in a condominium is given in Chapter 1; however, if you need specific help or advice regarding the current condominium rules and regulations, which are too numerous to be summarised here, you should contact the following association:

AIACI
Associazione Italiana Amministratori di Condomini e Immobili
Via Salandra 1/A
Rome
Tel: (06) 4746903.

In towns and cities where there is a student population you will also find *camere* (rooms) to rent, but do not expect them to be cheap or particularly easy to find, as the pressure of student numbers in the Italian university system means that what is available is often snapped up at above the odds prices. Suburban houses and villas to rent do exist, as do country properties, but they are much harder to come by.

FINDING A PLACE TO RENT

One way of finding a holiday let is to contact the local tourist board in the region that you wish to stay in. They will probably give you a list of properties which you can then phone or contact by writing. This is particularly convenient if you are in the UK and therefore have little opportunity to conduct your own research.

Those based in Britain should also look in the British Sunday newspapers, especially the *Sunday Times* and the *Sunday Telegraph*, which have good columns for holiday lets in Italy. The properties advertised here are often owned by British families, and so you are presented with none of the problems that you can meet telephoning an Italian landlord who only speaks Italian when you only speak English. It may also be worth contacting the Italian agencies below who deal with holiday lets and who will probably have English-speaking staff:

Interhome Srl
Via B. d'Alviano 71
20146 Milan
Tel: (02) 48302252.

Solemar Srl Via Cavour 80
50129 Florence
Tel: (055) 218112.

Cuendet & Cie Spa
Localita Il Cerreto Strove
53035 Monteriggione
Siena
Tel: (0577) 301012.

International House Brokers
Via Provaccini 7
20154 Milan
Tel: (02) 33609947.

Alternatively, look in Italian property journals and magazines, such as the property tabloid *Metroquadro* and its magazine edition of holiday lets, *Metroquadro Vacanze*. Subscriptions to both of these can be obtained at the following address:

ELI
Ufficio Abbonamenti
Via Anton Giulio Bragaglia 33
00123 Rome.

Holiday lets are also advertised in the glossy monthly magazines *Dove* and *Case di Class*. For subscriptions write to the following addresses respectively:

RCS—Rizzoli Periodici
Servizio Abbonamenti
Via Angelo Rizzoli 2
20132 Milan.

Case di Class
Ufficio Abbonamenti
Corso Italia 22
20122 Milan.

It is also worth scanning the *Affiti Turistici* columns in the local papers in the region you wish to stay, and looking out for the local versions of *Exchange & Mart*, of which there are many. One which comes out in regional editions weekly is called *Mercatino*.

The classified columns in newspapers and magazines are also a good place to search for longer-term rents. *Metroquadro* and *Dove* (see above for addresses) both have sections for longer-term rents as well as holiday lets.

Perhaps the more conventional approach is to go to a local *agenzia immobiliari*, preferably one that does not specifically state *compravendita*, which means that it mainly deals with property sales and purchases. Most estate agents have a good idea of what is available and what might be coming on to the market in the near future. They will also be able to give you an accurate picture of the market rates in the locality and advise you on contractual matters and so on.

If you find a reliable agent you may be able to leave a set of specifications for the type of rental you are seeking and an idea of the sort of price you are prepared to pay, so that he or she can pursue your search in your absence. However, as is normal practice in any country, agents will expect a percentage for their troubles, and it is a good idea to establish their terms at the very beginning of your dealings with them.

Another method is to walk the streets in the area in which you would like to live looking for **affittasi** or **da affitare** (to rent) signs in windows and on front doors, asking local inhabitants and shopkeepers if they know of any vacancies.

Below is a vocabulary list that may come in useful when reading the classified ads or chatting to housing agents. Further vocabulary related to the rooms and parts of a building is listed in the Glossary at the end of the book.

al mese	a month
ammobiliato	furnished
appartamento	flat
arredato	furnished
ascensore	lift
bilocale	two-room
breve periodo	short time
con gusto	tastefully
contratto	contract
disponibile	available
doppi servizi	two bathrooms
due piani	two floors
grattaciele	skyscraper
libero	unoccupied
lusso	luxury
mensile	monthly
mensilmente	every month
mesi estivi	summer months
mesi invernale	winter months
mesi primaveri	spring months
metri quadro (mq)	square metres
monolocale	one-room
ore pasti	meal times
ore seriali	evening times
parzialmente arredato	partially furnished
periodi vacanzie	holiday times
piano	floor
piano terra	ground floor

piu spesi	plus expenses
portineria	caretaker
posto letto	bed space
prezzo	price
primo piano	first floor
referenziati	with references
restaurato	restored
riscaldamento autonomo	independent heating
riscaldamento centrale	central heating
ristrutturato	restored
secondo piano	second floor
semi arredato	semi-furnished
servizi	services
settimanalmente	weekly
spese condominiali comprese	condominium expenses included
stagionalmente	in tourist season
signorile	distinguished
soggiorno	sitting room
telefono	telephone
termoautonomo	independent thermostat
uso transitorio	temporary use
villa	detached house
vista mare	sea view
vuoto	empty, unfurnished

TERMS, PRICES AND LETTING

Terms

Having found a place you would like to rent the next step is to negotiate the terms. This is extremely important and you should not be in any doubt as to exactly what you are and what you aren't liable for, not forgetting service charges and insurance, and so on. Rents are generally fixed at declared, set rates, but it may be worth trying to negotiate a lower rent in return for payment in undeclared cash, if this is possible. The deposit that you will have to put down is largely up to the owner's discretion, but is restricted by law to anything up to the value of three months' rent.

If you are renting in a condominium you will find you are subject to many rules and regulations which are all written down in a book. Ask to see the **regolamento** (rules), and read them yourself if your Italian is up to it, or have them explained to you in English. You may also request to

Object	Time/method	Owner	Tenant
Waterheater	Installation After first year of installation	100% 50%	50%
Hot water boiler in kitchen	After one year replacement or repair	50%	50%
Bathroom suite (e.g. bath, basin etc.)	Installation Replacement	100%	100%
Heating components (e.g. boiler, pipes etc.)	Installation Replacement	100% 50%	50%
Handles, locks, windows	Installation Replacement	100%	100%
Shutters, railings	Maintenance	100%	
Blinds	Replacement Maintenance with replacement of parts, e.g. straps, springs, hooks	100%	100%
Doors, windows	Gloss painting at start of tenancy; gloss painting after one year of start of tenancy	100%	100%
Internal walls	Decoration at start of tenancy; decoration one year after start of tenancy	100%	100%

Fig. 22. Liability for fixtures, fittings and general maintenance in condominium.

see the bill for the service charges of the previous year. It is a good idea to ask to see other previous bills too, e.g. for telephone, electricity, gas, so that you can be sure that they have been paid and that you are not taking on any debts.

The electricity and gas are more difficult to organise as bills are assessed according to the estimated consumption, with a rounding-up bill every year, or half year, to settle the difference between the real and estimated consumption. If the previous tenant or owner had a much larger consumption than you, you may find yourself paying large bills and perhaps not being around for the rebate when it arrives. This is something you should negotiate.

As a general outline Fig. 22 lists the fixtures, fittings and general maintenance for which you are liable as a tenant in a condominium and the proportion that is payable by the owner.

You may be interested to know that once you are settled in a rented flat you cannot be evicted except by court order and that harassment of tenants is strictly illegal.

Prices
Rents vary from town to town and are calculated according to the local land registry classification and the standard of the accommodation. Rents are fixed by the **Legge dell'Equo Canone**, the Rent Act that was passed in 1978 which also states that the minimum lease is for four years.

Fig. 23 gives the official rates for bedsit accommodation, two-room and three-room flats in central locations in some of the principal towns and cities in Italy. The prices, which are the cost of the rent per month, are given in millions of Italian lire. Remember that you may have to pay service charges on top of the basic rent.

Letting accommodation
If you wish to let out property yourself in Italy one of the best ways to find tenants for holiday lets is to advertise in British newspapers such as the *Sunday Times*, or put the property into the hands of a British villa agent. To find long-term tenants, advertise in the Italian property journal, *Metroquadro*, or in a local paper. It is equally possible to use a local **agenzia immobiliare** (estate agent).

As proprietor you are responsible for reporting the details of your tenants to the police. If the tenants are to stay in Italy for more than 30 days they will need to obtain a **Permesso di Soggiorno** (Permit to Stay) — see Chapter 5 (pages 117-123).

If you are letting out your property for more than three months you will

Place	Bedsit	2-room	3-room
Ancona	0.5	0.5–0.6	0.7–0.9
Aosta	0.6–0.7	0.8–1.0	1.2
Bari	0.4	0.6–0.7	1.2–1.5
Bergamo	0.6	0.9	1.2–1.3
Bologna	0.7–0.8	0.9–1.0	1.5
Bolzano	0.6	0.8–1.0	1.0
Brescia	—	0.7–1.0	0.8–1.0
Brindisi	0.5–0.6	0.6	0.6–0.7
Cagliari	—	0.9–1.0	0.9–1.0
Como	0.8–0.9	0.9–1.0	1.2–1.5
Cosenza	0.3	0.3	0.5–0.6
Cremona	0.4–0.5	0.5	0.7–0.8
Ferrara	0.5	0.7	1.0
Florence	0.8	1.0	1.2
Genoa	1.0–1.5	1.8	2.0
Isernia	0.4	0.5–0.6	0.7–0.8
Lecce	0.7–0.8	0.9	0.9–1.0
Lecco	—	0.9	0.9
Lucca	0.6–0.7	0.9	1.0–1.2
Macerata	0.4–0.5	0.6	0.7–0.8
Mantua	0.6	0.8–0.9	1.0
Milan	1.5	2.0	1.8–3.0
Modena	0.5–0.7	0.8–0.9	1.0–1.2

Fig. 23. Official rates for bedsits and flats in principal towns and cities.

Place	Bedsit	2-room	3-room
Naples	0.7–0.8	1.0–1.1	1.5–2.0
Padua	0.9	0.9	0.9–2.2
Palermo	0.6	0.8–0.9	0.8–1.3
Parma	0.5–0.8	0.7–0.8	1.0–1.2
Perugia	0.6	0.7	1.2
Pescara	—	0.7–0.8	1.1–1.2
Piacenza	0.3–0.4	0.4–0.5	0.7
Pisa	0.6	0.8–0.9	1.2–1.5
Pistoia	0.5–0.7	0.6–0.7	0.7–0.8
Prato	0.6–0.7	0.7	0.9–1.0
Ravenna	0.6–0.8	0.8–0.9	0.8–0.9
Rimini	0.5	0.5	0.7–0.8
Rome	1.0–1.2	1.7–1.8	2.7–2.8
Sassari	0.5	0.6–0.7	0.9–1.0
Siena	0.6–0.8	0.8–1.0	1.0–1.2
Syracuse	0.5–0.6	0.7–0.9	0.9–1.0
Trento	0.5–0.6	0.8	0.8–0.9
Treviso	0.4–0.5	0.7–0.8	0.9–1.0
Trieste	—	0.4–0.6	0.6–1.0
Turin	0.6–0.7	0.7–0.8	0.9–1.0
Venice	0.7–0.8	0.8–1.0	1.5–1.6
Verona	0.5–1.0	0.8–1.3	from 1.2
Vicenza	—	0.9	1.3
Viterbo	0.4–0.5	0.5	0.8

Fig. 23. Continued.

be subject to the **Equo Canone** (Fair Rent Act). This is enough to occupy a book in itself.

One of the principal complications in complying with the Equo Canone is in assessing the cost of your property per square metre which determines the rent you are allowed to charge. The first figure to take is the basic cost per square metre according to the year in which the property was constructed and also as to whether the property is in north–central Italy or south Italy. Fig. 24 shows the relevant figures (page 69).

This figure must then be multiplied by no less than seven variables, each of which is divided into relevant coefficient numbers which are too lengthy to be included here, but are issued by ISTAT (Istituto Nazionale di Statistica) and can be obtained at your local tax office. The basic variables are as below:

1. the type of habitation according to the cadastral registry (see above);
2. the population number of the local *comune*;
3. the location;
4. the floor on which you live (only applicable to apartment blocks with over three floors);
5. grade of property according to year of construction;
6. state of conservation and maintenance; and
7. additional percentage according to year of construction.

The result of these variables multiplied by the basic cost gives the square metre value of the property. This must then be multiplied by the area of the property. The area of the property is another calculation that sounds easier than it in fact is. The 'real' area is something quite different to the 'superficial' area which is the one that interests the tax office.

The superficial area is dependent on varying factors such as garages, balconies and minimum and maximum thresholds each of which has a coefficient number. Again these tables are available at your local tax office. Your final sum should then be divided by 3.85 per cent which gives you the annual **equo canone** (fair rent). For example, an apartment which has a total value of 30 million lire has a rental value of 1,155,000 per annum.

Apart from the headache of the *equo canone* other foibles of letting your home are fairly predictable. Among general damages, the telephone is something to be wary of, and remember that even if you remove the telephone, the socket is still available to plug in a portable phone. There isn't much you can do about this except to vet your future tenants as thoroughly as possible and ask for a large deposit to cover damages.

Year	North–central	South
Before 31/12/75	250,000	225,000
1976	285,000	260,000
1977	325,000	300,000
1978	370,000	340,000
1979	430,000	395,000
1980	500,000	460,000
1981	580,000	530,000
1982	680,000	620,000
1983	770,000	700,000
1984	840,000	765,000
1985	900,000	820,000
1986	930,000	850,000
1987	970,000	890,000
1988	1,030,000	950,000
1989	1,090,000	1,010,000
1990	1,155,000	1,070,000

Fig. 24. Cost of property per square metre in north, central
and south Italy, 1975–90.

3
Buying Property

LOOKING FOR A PROPERTY

How to find properties for sale

In Italy properties for sale are dealt with by *agenzie immobiliare* (estate agents), most of which are run on a very small scale. Many are franchises of nationwide organisations such as Tecnocasa or Grimaldi, but there is no real chain of estate agencies which makes for a rather parochial service. At worst the Italian *agenzia* is a fusty top-floor office, piled high with folders and pieces of paper, and a sign on the door saying *torno subito* (back soon). Even at best you are unlikely to come away bristling with details of properties to muse over at your leisure.

The system tends to be for you to describe the type of property you are looking for, name your price bracket and then follow the agent on a wild goose chase around the area in which you are interested. This is time-consuming, not only because of the travelling involved, but because keys often have to be hunted down and in many cases the agent hasn't really understood what you are looking for. The local *agenzia* is best consulted when you are looking for regular modern housing or even a plot of land on which to build, because as a general rule they are not accustomed to the hairbrained British in search of a semi-derelict country house to renovate.

A more professional service in properties to renovate and also those ready-restored is offered by British agencies who usually advertise in the property columns of the British Sunday newspapers. It is a good idea to contact these agencies at the outset of your search for an Italian property in order to be put on their mailing list. This will give you an idea of availability and going rates even if you do not find your dream home. If you go ahead with a property, you should be warned that British agents often try to rake off a commission from both the buyer and the seller at well above the odds. Therefore check the terms before making any commitments.

If you are in any doubt as to the credential of any estate agent based in Italy you can check that they are registered with the local **Camera di Commercio** (Chamber of Commerce). An estate agent is required by Italian law to be properly qualified and registered, and if they are not, they cannot receive commission or any other form of fee. Indeed, if they are not, they may well be acting illegally and if found out they would be penalised.

Other ways of finding property if you are already in Italy include searching through the classified advertisements in local newspapers and also in the monthly property journal, *Metroquadro* which can be subscribed to by contacting the following address:

Metroquadro
Edizioni Living International srl
Via Anton Giulio Bragaglia 33
00123 Rome
Tel: (06) 3788224.

Rather more prestigious properties are advertised in the monthly glossy magazine, *Villa e Casale*, which can be subscribed to at the same address as that for *Metroquadro* (see above), and also the glossy monthly magazines *Dove* and *Case di Class*, subscriptions to which are available at the following addresses respectively:

Dove
RSC—Rizzoli Periodici
Servizio Abbonamenti
Via Angelo Rizzoli 2
20132 Milan.

Case di Class
Ufficio Abbonamenti
Corso Italia 22
20122 Milan.

A wide range of properties for sale are also advertised in the monthly magazine *Tecnocasa*. *For subscription details contact one of the following regional offices:*

ILFI Unita Locale Torino (Piedmont)
Via Cibrario 6
Turin
Tel: (011) 4730549.

ILFI Assago (Lombardy)
Via Einstein 3
Milan
Tel: (02) 45701017.

Centro Servizi (Veneto)
Via Albere 29
Verona
Tel: (045) 577336.

Centro Servizi (Emilia Romagna)
Via Indipendenza 23
Bologna
Tel: (051) 220295.

Centro Servizi (Lazio)
Via Triburtina 654/A
Rome
Tel: (06) 4392148.

Tecnocasa as well as producing a magazine are a franchise company that is represented by some 500 housing agents, most of which are concentrated in northern Italy and in and around Rome. It may be worth contacting a Tecnocasa agent to find out the type of property with which they deal and the services that they offer. In addition to the addresses above, the following are the addresses of Tecnocasa agents in principle cities in other regions in Italy:

Novoli
Via Tagliaferri 6
Florence
Tel: (055) 4222718.

Isolotto
Via Cecioni 102
Florence
Tel: (055) 7398072.

Via M. della Resistenza 82
Ancona
Tel: (071) 2801230.

Vomero 1
Via Cilea 269
Naples
Tel: (081) 7141305.

Vomero 2
Piazza Leonardo 11
Naples
Tel: (081) 5781127.

Vomero 3
Via E. Jannelli 78
Naples
Tel: (081) 5605801.

Poggio Franco
Viale Concilio Vaticano 11
Bari
Tel: (080) 5041723.

Via Fata Morgana 9
Messina
Sicily
Tel: (090) 344908.

There is a property databank that can be consulted free of charge, by dialling the *numeroverde* 1678 61135. Another property databank is Telecasa at the following address:

Viale Bastioni di Michelangelo 5/A
00192 Roma
Tel: (06) 39723173.

A final alternative to searching for a property in Italy is to hunt around in the area in which you are interested, talking to the locals and if you are in a rural area going to the local *comune* or *municipio* (town hall). Someone in the town hall, usually a surveyor or architect, will give you a run-down on local properties that are for sale and may also offer to take you around to see them.

Property jargon

While searching for a property you are most probably going to have to rely on your Italian, unless you are in British-dominated Tuscany. Your phrase book or pocket dictionary will not get you very far for, as with all property markets, there is a special jargon. The following is a list of property jargon and vocabulary, while words related to houses and the parts of houses are listed in the glossary at the end of the book.

abitabile	habitable
accessibilita	accessibility
acqua di sorgente	spring water
acquedotto comunale	municipal water system
adatto	suitable for
ammirevole	admirable
ampia metratura	ample size
annessi	attached
antico	antique
a posto	everything in order
arredato	furnished
astenersi agenzie	without an agent
attacate	joined
attrezzata	equipped
belissima	beautiful
ben conservata	well-conserved
ben tenuto	well-maintained
borgo	hamlet
bosco	wood
buona posizione	good position
buono stato	good condition
cancello eletrico	electric gate
caratteristico	typical
casa d'epoca	period house
centralissimo	very central
centro storico	historic centre
circondata da	surrounded by
comodissimo mezzi e negozi	convenient location for public transport and shops
complesso residenziale	residential complex
composto da	composed of
condominio	condominium
consegna	exchange contracts

coppi vecchi	old roof tiles
da restaurare	to be restored
da ricostruire	to be reconstructed
da rifare	to be done
da ristrutturare	to be restored
da sistemare	to be put in order
doppi vetri	double glazing
entroterra	hinterland
facciata	façade
finiture lusso	luxury finish
forno a legna	wood-burning oven
fronte mare	sea-facing
grezzo	uncut stone
ha	hectare
impareggiabile	incomparable
imprendibile	unbelievable
incantevole	charming
in corso di costruzione	in the process of being constructed
in corso di ristrutturazione	in the process of being restored
in parte ristruturrato	partly restored
in ordine	in order
libero	unoccupied
luce	electricity
marmi	marble
mattone	brick
metrature	size
metro quadro (mq)	square metre
mutuo compresso	mortgage included
nuova	new
occasione esclusiva	exclusive bargain
oliveto	olive grove
ottima posizione	excellent position
ottime condizione	excellent condition
ottime finiture	excellent finish
ottimo stato	excellent condition
paese	village
paesino	small village
pagamento	payment
pavimenti in cotto	terracotta tiling

perfette condizioni	perfect condition
permutasi con	in exchange with
piccolo	small
pietra-legno originali	original stone and wood
poggio	hill
posto auto	parking space
prestigioso	prestigious
prezzo	price
progetti approvati	approved plans
pronta consegna	ready to exchange contract
riscaldamento autonomo	independent heating
ristrutturato	restored
rudere	ruin
servizi allacciati	services connected
signorile	distinguished
soffiti a volta	vaulted ceilings
spese agenzia	agent's fees
spiaggia	beach
strada	road
strutturalmente	structurally
subito	straight away
telefono	telephone
termoautonomo	independent thermostat
terreno	land
terreno alberato	land with trees
terreno boschivo	wooded land
terreno coltivate	cultivated land
terreno circostante	surrounded by land
terreno per orto	land for vegetable plot
trattativa	negotiation
trattabili	negotiable
travi di legno	wooden beams
travi a vista	exposed beams
vecchio	old
viale privato	private road
vicino stazione ferroviaria	railway station nearby
vigneto	vineyard
vista mare	sea view
vista monti	mountain view
zona collinare	hilly area
zona tranquilla	peaceful area

Points to consider before buying

Once you have found a property you should make sure that you really know what you are taking on before making any commitments. The first point to take into consideration is the location. A property that looks idyllic in the summer months may be buried beneath snow, flooded by a river or blocked from the sun winter long. It may be inaccessible in bad weather and it may also be difficult to heat, especially if there is a problem with the damp.

The second point to consider is: what are the amenities? Is there a road, electricity and water? Find out how many metres it is to the nearest mains electricity and water source. The cost of connecting these services, roads included, is usually priced per metre and will be an expense that you will need to take into consideration before agreeing to the selling price.

You should also take into consideration the cost of restoration if it is necessary. Unless you are prepared to do the work yourself you will pay a considerable sum for builders. You will also find that building materials, particularly wood, are more expensive in Italy than in the UK. So do not be fooled into thinking that a low purchase price will translate into a low restoration price.

In fact one of the reasons that derelict rural property is cheap in some parts of Italy is that it is recognised that the restoration is prohibitively expensive, and therefore the property is less desirable and saleable. This is partly why Italians show little interest in derelict properties, preferring to invest their money in building a new villa. Building afresh with modern building materials is somewhat cheaper than knocking down and rebuilding using original materials.

THE BUYING PROCESS

The *notaio*

Once you have found a property you will need to contact a **notaio** (notary), the public official responsible for drawing up the deeds (**rogito**) and registering the transfer of property. It is customary for the buyer to choose the *notaio*, unless you are purchasing a flat in a condominium or a plot on a new housing development, as the buyer is usually responsible for paying their fee. They are listed in the *Pagine Gialle* (Yellow Pages) under *Notai*, although as a foreigner you will most probably be recommended one, either by the agent or vendor. There is no need to be wary of taking a recommendation as the *notaio* is impartial and acts equally for both parties involved. The only point you may wish to look into are the fees as they vary from place to place, ranging from 1 to 2 per cent of the purchase price.

Searches and surveys

The first step in the buying process is for the *notaio* to make searches into the ownership of the property in question. This is to ensure the legitimacy of the seller and also to check that there is no mortgage or other payment outstanding. At the same time a **geometra** should be employed to carry out a survey (for more on this see Chapter 4, p. 94). If you are planning on converting or changing the property in any way you should check at this stage with the *geometra* that it is possible. For example, in some regions it is not possible to get permission for a swimming pool due to limited water supplies.

You will also come up against local building regulations. For instance, unless your house is in a village, you will not get permission to convert a room with a ceiling height of under 2.7 m into a living space. Another common scenario is the difficulty in converting a property that is registered as agricultural into a holiday home. If this is the case, you should arrange for the vendor to apply for a de-ruralisation certificate from the local authorities.

The *geometra* should also inform you as to any public rights of way or access on your property. Known as **servitu di passagio**, these rights include access to a well or water source. The rights can be one of two types, either permanent or renewable every twenty years. In the latter case you can refuse to grant permission when it comes to being renewed.

It is also important for the *geometra* to inform you of any public works that are projected, such as roads, electricity lines and so on, that would affect the property. If you are buying a historic building ask the *geometra* to find out if it is listed, in which case there will be restrictions over its use and also its future sale. Now is also the time, if you are buying a flat in a condominium, to get hold of the condominium rule book, **regolamento di condominio**, to check that you can live according to the conditions set out.

If either the searches or the survey reveal any defects or you have any doubts about the property it is still possible to withdraw from the proceedings and simply pay the fees for the *notaio* and *geometra* that have so far been incurred.

The compromesso

If you are still happy with the property then the next step is to go ahead with the preliminary contract. While this is being drawn up you should obtain a **Codice Fiscale**, an Italian Fiscal Code number (see Chapter 5 for application procedure). The *Codice Fiscale* will need to be presented at all further meetings with the *notaio* (as well as a passport or identity card).

You will also need a *Codice Fiscale* in order to open a bank account, which you will probably be doing in order to transfer money for the purchase.

The preliminary contract, the **compromesso**, is a significant commitment and involves the payment of a deposit towards the property as an act of goodwill. The purpose of the *compromesso* is to clarify all the conditions of the sale, including the price and terms of payment.

It is an old practice to declare a lower price on the contract than that actually paid in order to avoid registration tax on behalf of the buyer and income tax on behalf of the seller. Whether you choose to do this or not, you should remember that you too will be liable to pay tax when you come to sell on the property. You should also note that it will be considered highly suspicious should you declare a price that is actually lower than the minimum statutory value according to the local land registry (**catasto**).

It is very important that the buyer does not sign the *compromesso* until he is perfectly happy with everything written in the contract. Remember that the buyer is in a position to impose conditions or restrictions on the vendor at this stage. Buyers should also be sure that if they are buying a property with a mortgage it is clearly stated that the purchase will only be completed subject to the confirmation from the mortgage or housing loan company. Once the contract has been signed there is no going back.

The signing of the *compromesso*, which involves both the vendor and buyer, or their attorneys, must take place in the presence of the *notaio*. At the time of signing the buyer must pay a deposit of between 10 and 30 per cent of the sale price. If the buyer does not go through with the purchase after signing the *compromesso*, they will lose the deposit that has been paid and may be sued by the vendor. If, however, the sale does not proceed because of the vendor then the buyer has the right to demand up to twice the amount of the deposit paid in compensation. In this case the buyer may not only be able to claim damages but may also have the sale compulsorily completed by court order.

If there is any doubt in the mind of either the buyer or the vendor as to the final completion of the sale, it is possible to state in the *compromesso* that the deposit is withdrawable, **caparra penitenziale**. This will prevent any further legal proceedings or claims for damages. However, in the case of the buyer's breaking the contract he or she will still have to lose the deposit to the vendor, and in the case of the vendor's withdrawing he or she will still have to pay double the deposit amount to the buyer.

On the other hand if both the seller and buyer want a quick sale and have no differences concerning conditions, price or otherwise, it is possible to have the actual transfer of the property written into the *compromesso.* The only formality required after this is for the document to be officially registered.

The *atto*

The normal procedure after signing the *compromesso* is to meet again on the agreed completion date to exchange contracts, a procedure known as the **atto**. This is also carried out in the presence of the *notaio* who should in the mean time have rechecked the ownership of the property and any outstanding payments and have drawn up a title deed, the **rogito**. The *notaio* reads out the final contract aloud and then certifies the signatures of the buyer and seller, or, in the case of either one of their absences, by **procura speciale** (power of attorney). The *notaio* will then ask the buyer to pay the fees incurred and also the taxes that are due.

You will also have to pay the purchase price of the property to the seller. Once monies are transferred and the title deed is signed, the property has officially changed hands, although the *notaio* still has to register the title deed at the *catasto* (land registry). Your copy of the certified title deed will be ready for collection or delivery after about two months.

If after inspecting your property you find that it does not meet the stipulations on the contract or that there are some undisclosed defects, the buyer should contact the seller within eight days of signing the *atto*. If it is necessary to take court action, legal proceedings must be started within one year of signing the *atto*.

MONEY MATTERS

Purchase taxes

The first type of tax you will pay having bought a property in Italy is registration tax, **Imposta di Registro**. According to the law of 15 February 1992, number 1896, the amount of tax you pay depends on if it is your first and only home. If it is your first home you are eligible for the reduced tax of 4 per cent of the property value. If it is your second home then you are liable to pay the full registration tax of 10 per cent. Registration tax for agricultural land is 17 per cent. The percentage is calculated according to the price of the property as declared on the title deed.

You will also have to pay **IVA** (VAT) at 19 per cent of the price declared on the title deed. If you are the builder of the property you have purchased then you are eligible for a reduced *IVA* (VAT) rate of 4 per cent. You are also eligible for a reduced registration tax levied at a flat rate of 200,000Lit.

Property taxes

Italian property tax, which is paid annually, usually in June or July, has changed very frequently in Italy over recent years, partly because the Finance Ministry have been continually trying to eliminate tax evaders, and partly because they have been trying to maximise the income into the state's bankrupt coffers. At last some sort of a final form seems to have been reached.

The former Italian capital gains tax, INVIM *(Imposta Comunale sull'Incremento degli Immobili)* and the local income tax ILOR *(Imposta Locale sui Redditi)* have been replaced by a council tax, ICI *(Imposta Comunale sugli Immobili)*. ICI is to be paid by anyone owning, or having rights to, property or land in Italy whether they are resident or non-resident. It is an annual tax amounting to 0.4–0.7 per cent of the value of your property according to the **rendita catastale** (cadastral income) as set by the land registry. If the property is dilapidated or unfit for habitation then you will pay only 50 per cent of the tax levied.

The classifications of housing as formulated by the *catasto* (land registry) appear on your property deeds and are as listed below, but to find out your *rendita catastale* you must take your title deed to your local cadastral office, or employ an agent to do so on your behalf.

A/1 Abitazione di tipo signorile
    Exclusive housing

A/2 Abitazione di tipo civile
    Civilian housing

A/3 Abitazione di tipo economico
    Economical housing

A/4 Abitazione di tipo popolare
    Working class housing

A/5 Abitazione di tipo ultrapopolare
    Ultra working class housing

A/6 Abitazione di tipo rurale
    Rural housing

A/7 Abitazione in villini
    Small detached housing

A/8 Abitazione in ville
Detached housing

A/9 Castelli, palazzi di eminenti pregi artistici o storici
Castle or building of eminent historic or artistic importance

A/10 Uffici e studi privati
Private offices and studios

A/11 Abitazione o alloggi tipici dei luoghi
Housing or accommodation typical of the region

As with all tax in Italy you are well advised to employ a **commercial-ista** (accountant) or an agent to oversee your payments. The form to fill in for ICI is complicated even for Italians, let alone for someone without the full command of the Italian language. An accountant will not only complete the necessary paperwork but you can probably arrange for him to pay the tax on your behalf in the case of your absence.

It is important to keep tax payments up to date partly because you will be fined if found out, and partly because you will find problems in selling your house as the outstanding payments will come to light when searches are made. The fine for not paying ICI is issued in the form of additional tax, **sopratassa**, levied at 20–30 per cent of the amount due, with an interest rate of 6 per cent for every six months that the tax is left unpaid.

You will also have to pay the tax known as IRPEF (*Imposta Sui Redditi Personale e Fisiche*). Again this is calculated according to the *rendita catastale*. There are minimum thresholds which you may find you fall below in which case you will have nothing to pay. The *rendita catastale* that exceeds this threshold is taxed on a sliding scale ranging from 20 to 50 per cent.

A word of warning. If you have a property in a town that remains unoccupied and not rented out you will be liable to pay taxes at a much higher rate. The same is true if it is your second home.

Other costs

Your property in Italy will accrue annual bills for communal services and water. *Servizio Riscossione Tributi Ruoli* (communal services) include rubbish collections and street lighting as well as general maintenance and repairs to public areas. The amount you pay depends how far you are from the nearest *comune*, but your annual bill is unlikely to exceed £100. The receipt for the bill, which you should always keep, gives a breakdown of the charges (see Fig. 25).

Your water bill is calculated according to a meter reading which someone from the Gestione Servizio Idrico (Water Board) will come to read once a year. The amount you pay will depend on the amount of water you consume. Again, an average household is unlikely to pay more than £100 per year. The bill receipt gives a breakdown of the charges (see Fig. 26).

If you have just bought your house then go to the *ufficio ragioniera* (accounts department) at your local *comune* or *municipio* (town hall) to inform them of the change in ownership. Once you are entered on the computer, bills will automatically be sent to you and must be paid at the post office or a bank. If you are not a full-time resident and bills are left lying on your doormat, do not worry: drastic action is not usually taken against tardy payment.

There is also a new tax in the pipeline called ISCOM (*Imposta Servizio Comunale*), which will be a tax on communal services.

Loans and mortgages

Mutui (loans or **Mutui ipotecarie** (mortgages) for buying property can be arranged through an Italian bank or a credit company for up to 75 per cent of the value of the property. The main banks and credit companies dealing with loans and mortgages in Italy are as follows:

Banca Nazionale dell'Agricoltura	Tel: (06) 85881
Banca Nazionale del Lavoro	Tel: (06) 51703434
Banco di Napoli	Tel: (081) 7911111
Banco di Sicilia	Tel: (091) 587933
Carical Lucania	Tel: (0984) 8011
Carigenova	Tel: (010) 20911
Caripol	Tel: (02) 88661
Carispaq	Tel: (0862) 6491
Caritorino	Tel: (011) 6921
Credito Fondiario e Industriale	Tel: (06) 5796
Efibanca	Tel: (06) 85991
Italfondiario	Tel: (06) 47791
Montipaschi	Tel: (0577) 294111
San Paolo	Tel: (011) 5551
UCB-Credicasa	Tel: (02) 676021

It is also possible to take out a loan with a British building society. The Woolwich who offer mortgages of up to 80 per cent of the value of the

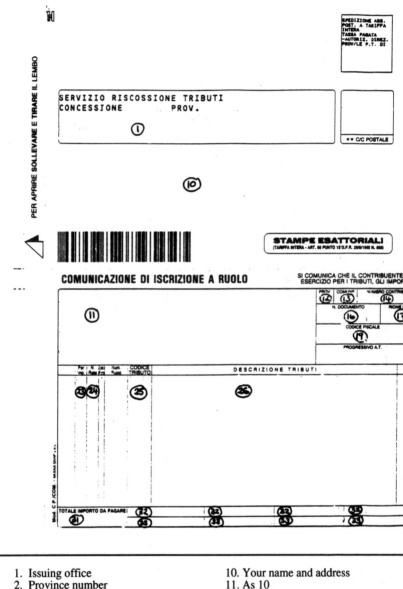

Fig. 25. Bill for communal services

1. Issuing office
2. Province number
3. Commune number
4. Tax payer's number
5. Document number
6. Area number
7. Group number
8. Emission number
9. Fiscal tax code number
10. Your name and address
11. As 10
12. As 2
13. As 3
14. As 4
15. As 8
16. As 5
17. As 6
18. Delivery date

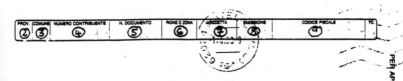

| PROV. | COMUNE | NUMERO CONTRIBUENTE | N. DOCUMENTO | RIONE O ZONA | MAZZETTA | EMISSIONE | CODICE FISCALE | TC |
| ② | ③ | ④ | ⑤ | ⑥ | ⑦ | ⑧ | ⑨ | |

PER APRIRE SOLLEVARE E TIRARE IL LEMBO

IMPOSTA DI BOLLO ASSOLTA IN MODO VIRTUALE-AUT.INTEND.DI FINANZA
DI   N.   DEL

IL CARICATO È ISCRITTO NEI RUOLI DEL CORRENTE
CON LE SCADENZE QUI DI SEGUITO EVIDENZIATE:

VEDERE A TERGO LE AVVERTENZE
NON STACCARE LA PARTE SUPERIORE

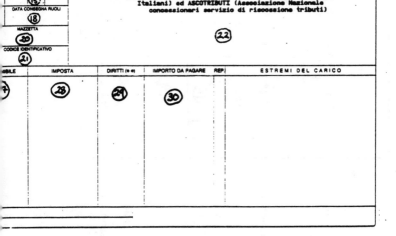

| ESERC. | EMIS. | T.° | COMUNICATO a cura di ANCI (Associazione Nazionale Comuni Italiani) ed ASCOTRIBUTI (Associazione Nazionale concessionari servizio di riscossione tributi) |
| ⑮ | | | |

DATA CONSEGNA RUOLI ⑱

MAZZETTA ⑳

CODICE IDENTIFICATIVO ㉑

㉒

| ...IBILE | IMPOSTA | DIRITTI (e e) | IMPORTO DA PAGARE | REP. | ESTREMI DEL CARICO |
| ㉗ | ㉘ | ㉙ | ㉚ | | |

19. As 9
20. As 7
21. Identification code
22. Customer advice notes
23. Tax year
24. Rate number
25. Tax code
26. Description of service taxable
27. Amount liable to tax

28. Tax
29. Law
30. Amount payable
31. Total amount payable
32. Pay-by dates for payment in instalments
33. Amount payable in each instalment

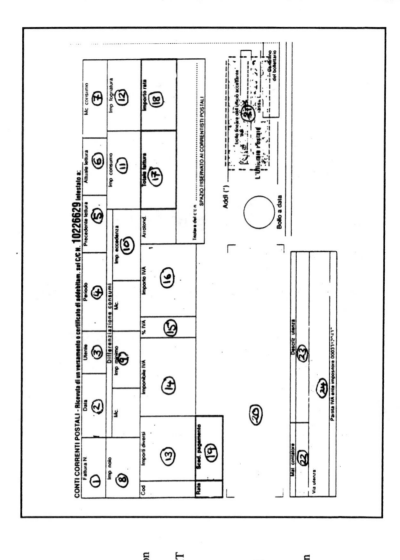

1. Bill number
2. Date
3. Consumer
4. Period covered
5. Previous reading
6. Actual reading
7. Amount consumed
8. Hire charge
9. Minimum charge
10. Surplus charge
11. Charge for consumption
12. Sewerage
13. Other
14. Amount subject to VAT
15. VAT percentage
16. Amount of VAT
17. Total bill
18. Amount payable by instalment
19. Pay-by-date
20. Consumer's name and address
21. Stamp that bill is paid
22. Meter registration
23. Consumer's description
24. Consumer's address

Fig. 26. Water bill (receipt)

property, and Abbey National who offer mortgages of up to the value of 85 per cent, have offices in Italy at the following addresses:

Woolwich SPA
Via degli Omenoni 2
20121 Milan
Tel: (02) 8690704.

Abbey National Mutui SPA
Via Dante 16
20121 Milan
Tel: (02) 846891.

In order to apply for a mortgage you will need to supply the following documents:

1. full address of property;
2. draft sale agreement of property;
3. photocopy of identity document;
4. photocopy of last tax return (Modello 740 or 101);
5. survey report carried out by registered surveyor;
6. *stato di famiglia* (available from *comune*);
7. *certificato di residenza* (available from *comune*)
8. photocopy of *Codice Fiscale*.

If you have not already had a survey carried out, in the case of Abbey National they will arrange to have this done for you at an approximate fee of 300,000Lit.

The mortgage contract is usually completed at the same time as the *atto*, the final purchase. The purchaser, vendor, *notaio* and probably an attorney from the mortgage company will have to be present. Once it is signed the mortgage contract must be registered at the land registry and a registration tax is levied at 2 per cent of the sum financed plus interest and plus a flat rate of 200,000Lit. It will also be necessary to pay the notary a separate fee for this which will be calculated according to a percentage of the sum financed. Below is the type of bill you can expect to pay for taking out a mortgage for the value of 30 million Lire.

Survey	Lit.	300,000
Stamp duties	Lit.	1,200,000
Registration tax	Lit.	720,000
Flat rate registration tax	Lit.	200,000
Notary fees	Lit.	1,500,000
Insurance against fire	Lit.	154,000

You may buy property that is already mortgaged, in which case you will be expected to take it over on purchase. It is important therefore to find out exactly what mortgage payments remain to be paid in order to deduct them from the purchase price.

Insurance

The moment property passes into your hands you should arrange to take out insurance. The basic insurance only covers **incendio ed altri danni ai beni** (fire and damage). For an added premium you can have **furto** (theft) added to the policy, but check the small print as payments are reduced by 50 per cent or more if your property does not meet the requirements of security outlined in the policy, such as bars on windows less than 3 metres from the ground. It is probably worth going to two or three insurance agents to get quotes and also find out the terms of claims.

Most policies work on a **franchigia** basis which means a flat cost is deducted from the compensation. Otherwise you get a percentage in return with a maximum usually stated. It is important to find a policy that suits you as once it is signed you are generally obliged to renew it annually for ten years. If you wish to withdraw from an insurance policy it is necessary to give six months' notice.

Below is a vocabulary list that will help you in talking to insurance brokers and reading up on the small print.

acqua condotta	water piping
apparcchiature	appliances
arredamento	furnishings
assicurato	insured party
assicurazione	insurance
assicurazione contro i terzi	third-party insurance
atti vandalici	vandalisation
azione del fulmine	lightning damage
bang sonico	sonic boom
buffera	storm

caduta di aeromobili	aeroplane crash
contenuto dell' abitazione	house contents
contraente	contracting party
cose rubate	stolen goods
danni a terzi	damage to third party
danni eletrici	electrical damages
danno	damage
denuncia	statement
dolo	fraud
esplosione	explosion
fulmine	lightning
fuoriuscita di liquidi	leakage of liquids
furto	theft
grandine	hailstorms
guasti	breaking and entry
incendio	fire
indennizzo	compensation
mobilio	furniture
oggetti pregiati	valuable objects
oggetti preziosi	precious objects
pagamento	payment
perdita delle pigioni	loss of rent
polizza globale abitazione	global policy for house
polizza globale fabbricati	global policy for building
premio	premium
rimborso	reimbursement
risarcimento	compensation
riparazione	repair
rischio	risk
rottura accidentale delle lastre	accidental breakage of window panes
rottura	breakage
scippo	theft
scoppio	explosion
sinistri	accidents
sommosse	uprising
spargiamento d' acqua	water explosion
spese	expenses
sviluppo di gas/fumo/vapori	gas/smoke/fume leak
tempeste	tempest
trombe d' aria	whirlwind

tumulti	riot
uragani	hurricane
urto di veicoli stradali	crash from road vehicle
valore	value
vento	wind

4
Renovating

MAKING PLANS

Architects

To renovate a house in Italy you may need at some point to employ an architect. You can employ an architect to oversee the entire project, which means making plans from reconstruction to furnishings, and includes getting estimates and being regularly on site to direct the work. Alternatively you may wish to employ an architect only to draw up plans for projects and have them approved by the local *comune* (town hall).

The architect's fee is generally calculated according to the total estimated amount of the work to be done on a property. If you are employing an architect full-time, you can expect to pay between 3,300,000 and 3,800,000Lit. on work valued at 20,000,000. For work valued at 30,000,000 you can expect to pay an architect somewhere between 4,700,000 and 5,300,000Lit., and for work valued at 40,000,000Lit. the architect will charge between 5,800,000 and 6,600,000Lit. etc.

The architect fees for simply drawing up plans are somewhat less. For work valued at 20,000,000Lit. the architect receives between 1,900,000 and 2,200,000Lit. On a job estimated to be worth 30,3000,000Lit. the architect will ask from 2,600,000 to 3,000,000Lit, and for an estimate of 40,000,000Lit. the architect will charge between 3,300,000 and 3,800,000Lit.

Other professionals you may wish to employ at the plan-making stage include the *geometra* There is no exact equivalent of the *geometra* in Britain, the nearest being a surveyor. The job of a *geometra* is to draw up plans for existing property rather than designing something new. This is not to say, however, that the *geometra* does not draw up plans for new projects, but that a *geometra* would not be the person to employ were you to build a house from scratch.

If the renovation you are undertaking involves only minor modifications or the restoration of an old property you may well prefer to employ a *geometra* as they can survey the property at the same time. As a general rule the *geometra* tends to be more practical and may have better contacts in the building trade than the architect. Like the architect, the *geometra* can either partake in the entire project from start to finish, or can be employed for one function only.

Applying for reduced rate of VAT

Before buying any materials for renovation or employing anyone, you should find out whether the project you are undertaking is eligible for the reduced rate of *IVA* (VAT) at 4 per cent as opposed to the full rate of 19 per cent. If you are employing someone to carry out the work for you this means a reduction on the VAT that appears on their bill, although it will probably be your responsibility to arrange the official permission (see below on p. 94). If you are carrying out the building work yourself, provided you go through the correct application procedure, the reduction will apply to building materials, plumbing and so on.

Before applying for the **l'abbatimento dell'IVA** (reduction on VAT) you should find out if the work you wish to carry out is eligible. The list below contains the principal types of jobs that are eligible for reduced VAT.

1. *Manutenzione ordinaria* (routine maintenance: renovation, replacement of existing installations)
2. *Manutenzione straordinaria* (special maintenance: work and modifications needed to renovate or substitute parts of the building, including modernising bathrooms, providing that the dimensions of the building and its designated use are not changed)
3. *Restauro e di risanamento conservativo* (restoration and conservative redevelopment: works that restore a building to its former use and appearance)
4. *Ristrutturazione edilizia* (rebuilding: work to rebuild in a way that is different)

In order to apply you must write an official request both for permission to carry out the work and for a certificate that grants you 4 per cent IVA when purchasing materials specifically for the stated work. It should be addressed to the *sindaco* (local mayor) of your *comune* or *municipo*. The letter should be written on *carta semplice* (official lined paper) which has wide margins either side. It is the standard type of paper used in making any official transaction and can be bought by the sheet from a *tabaccherie* (tobacconists). Fig. 27 is a sample letter.

Al Sindaco del
Comune di [insert town]

OGGETTO: Richiesta autorizzazione per lo svolgomento
di lavoro de [insert type of work to be
done according to four headings given
above].

Il/la sottoscritto/a [your name] nato/a in [country in which
born] il [date of birth], resident in [name of local comune and
home address], dovendo procedere alla realizzazione di opera di
[insert type of work to be done according to four headings given
above] nel fabbricato sopradescritto consistente nel [describe
work to be done in detail]

CHIEDE

alla S.V. la autorizzazione per il lavoro di cui sopra.
Si richiede inoltre il rilascio di un certificato che atesto la
IVA al 4%
Distinti saluti

[write town/date/signature]

Fig. 27. Request for permission to carry out building work.

The official authorisation letter you receive in reply will look something like the one shown as Fig. 28.

Planning permission and building regulations

If you intend to make any major changes to your property you will have to apply for permission from your local *comune*. It is generally the work of a *geometra* to do this. The procedure basically involves the drawing up of plans, an application to the *comune*, and then the registration of the modification with the land registry. It is a fairly lengthy procedure, taking about two months to get the basics done, while it can take up to two years for the amended plans to be issued by the land registry.

It is also a somewhat costly business and you would be lucky to come away with a bill from a *geometra* of less than 1 million Lire for even the simplest job. It is none the less necessary, as building without permission can result in your having to demolish the illegal building as a **condono edilizio** (condemned building) and probably having a fine to pay. It will also cause problems when coming to sell the property as the ground plan will differ from that shown on the cadastral plan.

Planning permission is required for any structural modifications made to the exterior of a building, unless it is a wood-framed structure such as a pergola, a greenhouse or a garden shed. Agricultural properties are allowed greater freedom in planning permission which unfortunately means that hideous breeze-block barns often dominate lovely old farmsteads.

If you live in an urban area you will be expected to conform to the local colour scheme used in the painting of exterior walls. Find out from your local *comune* or *municipio* the range of colours that are allowed. Permission for changes to the interior is generally dealt with by **USL (Unita Sanitaria Locale)** who act on behalf of sanitation laws. Permission for interior alterations is not necessary, provided the changes are not drastic, that is you are not converting a pigsty into a bathroom, and that you follow the basic regulations:

- Structural walls must not be demolished.
- Enclosed kitchens must be at least 9 m2.
- Ceiling heights (except in villages) must be at least 2.7 m if the room is for habitation.

Any changes that you make to the use of land or property must be registered at the local land registry. Land and property are strictly classified in terms of use by the local land registry and it is not always easy to

Città di

PROT. N. :   Li,   ①

②

OGGETTO: ③

④ IL SINDACO

⑤ In riferimento alla istanza della S.V. in data
tendente ad ottenere il rilascio di autorizzazione per
eseguire i lavori di   nel
fabbricato sito in   consistenti nel

        ;

⑥ - Vista la legge   , n.   ;
   - Vista la legge   n.   , artt.   ;
   - Vista la legge   , n.   ;
   - Vista la legge   . n.   , art. ;

⑦ AUTORIZZA

                    , proprietaria del fabbricato sito
⑧ in   , ad eseguire i lavori di
         citati in premessa.-

            IL SINDACO

    ⑨

---

1. Date
2. Your name and address
3. Objectivity
4. The Mayor
5. With reference to your application dated (date) for authorisation to follow out the work for (type of work) in the building situated in (address) consisting of: (description of work)
6. Laws
7. Authorises
8. (Your name), owner of the building located in (address), to carry out the work of (type of work) above mentioned
9. The Mayor

Fig. 28. Authorisation letter.

achieve alterations. This should be thoroughly investigated before buying a property: if you fail to get the property reclassified it may well hinder your chances of purchasing it. One of the most common changes to property is from an agricultural status to that of residential or holiday home.

Making changes to land also needs planning permission in certain circumstances. Examples are building terraces in your garden, installing a swimming pool or building a new wall. Permission will be all the harder to obtain if you live in a place of touristic interest or on a **strada panoramica**.

Some general rules are:

- Never cut down a tree unless it is dead, and you can subsequently prove this was the case.
- Do not plant hedges less than 1.5 m from your neighbour's land.
- Do not put shadow on your neighbour's land.

Remember, projects that require permission should never be started until you have the **licenza** (permit) in your hand, and once you do you must make sure it is possible to complete the work before the planning permission date expires.

THE BUILDING TRADE

Employing builders, plumbers, electricians and decorators in Italy is a costly business. Before embarking on any major project you may wish to estimate just how much it will cost. Don't listen to workmen or architects who say it will cost *poco* (little) as it very rarely does. It would be more realistic for you to find out the going rates and insist on having a proper estimate for the job. The final bill will probably be reduced if you offer to pay cash without a receipt — although bear in mind that this is not legal. If you have work done in this way you may lose out on getting certificates and guarantees which are assets when it comes to selling your property.

The following section is a guide to prices and also to the professions within the building trade, each of which is listed alphabetically. The Italian for each profession is provided at the start of each section to enable you to locate the relevant people in the *Pagine Giallo* (Yellow Pages) if necessary. Note that the telephone numbers supplied in the Yellow Pages are generally home numbers, therefore call at mealtimes 12–2 pm or after 8 pm to be sure of catching the person you wish to speak to. Also, note that all the prices given in the following section are exclusive of *IVA* (VAT).

Builders

Muratore (builders) and *imprese di costruzione* (construction firms) usually estimate a job price, known as a **forfait**, or a price per square metre, a **misura**, which includes both materials and labour. If the job is impossible to estimate, for example if it is the restoration of a frescoed wall, then a price is charged per hour, a method of payment known as **in economia**. Alternatively, builders may charge a fixed rate per day in addition to the cost of materials.

The prices that follow include labour and materials and are calculated per square metre.

General overall reconstruction	2,000,000Lit.
Internal, non-structural wall	
brick (5.5 x 12 x 25 cm)	105,000Lit.
semi-hollow bricks (4.5 x 15 x 30 cm)	95,000Lit.
semi-hollow bricks (8–10 x 15 x 30 cm)	72,000Lit.
plaster board panels	55–65,000Lit.

Demolition work can also be calculated at a price per square metre according to the material to be demolished. The following prices do not include the removal of the rubble.

Demolition	
brick wall (10 cm thick)	18,000Lit.
brick wall (15 cm thick)	22,000Lit.
semi-hollow brick wall (16 cm)	16,000Lit.
composite stone/marble floor	60–70,000Lit.
ceramic tile floor	25–30,000Lit.

To have rubble and other material taken away you will pay up to 65,000Lit. for a three-wheeler van load (approximately 1 cubic metre), provided the distance travelled is within 10 km. A lorry charges 35,000 Lit. for 6 cubic metres taken for a distance of no more than 10 km.

The removal of bathroom suites can be priced per item as follows:

shower base	26,000Lit.
bath	54,000Lit.
toilet	24,000Lit.
washbasin	27,000Lit.

The removal of piping can also be estimated per metre. Taking out plumbing pipes costs around 3,600Lit. per metre, while waste pipes cost 4,300Lit. per metre.

Before employing builders you should not only get an estimate for the job, and preferably be shown a property where they have worked before to see the standard of their workmanship, but you should check that they are covered by third-party insurance against accidents.

Carpenters

Your local *falegname* (carpenter) will undoubtedly be very busy, and you will probably have to wait for your requirement to be seen to. The lack of DIY discount stores means that most Italians have doors, windows and shutters made to measure. You will not only have to place your order well in advance of the time you will be needing it, but you will also pay a fairly high price. For a window made in pine wood, you can expect to pay in the region of 400,000Lit. per square metre, inclusive of glass and fittings. A pine door costs approximately the same.

If you need a carpenter to come and work on your property you will pay between 27,600Lit. and 31,000Lit. per hour, depending on how specialised the carpentry is. Alternatively, you may negotiate a fixed price for the complete job.

Decorators

Imbianchini (painters, literally translated, whitewashers) and *decoratore* (decorators) usually estimate the cost of a job on a square metre basis. A guide to prices for both *verniciatura* (painting) *and carteggiatura* (wall-papering) are as follows (the prices are for the square metre and include the cost of the materials and labour):

non-washable emulsion	17,000Lit.
washable emulsion	21,000Lit.
gloss paint	50,000Lit.
textured paint	50–70.000Lit.
lining paper	6,500Lit.
washable paper	19,000Lit.
vinyl paper	25,000Lit.

Electricians

An *elletricista* or *installatore* (electrician) can be hired for between 30,000 and 35,000Lit. per hour, or per electrical point that is installed. A typical bill for having electricity installed in an apartment with an area of 100 square metres would be in the region of 5,000,000Lit. Professional electricians should be registered at your local chamber of commerce, or associated to an organised body such as Uane, the telephone number of which is:

(02) 27001543

If an electrician is completely rewiring your house, ask for a certificate for the work done which can be presented when you come to sell your house. If you are building a new house you will need to show this certificate to the town hall in order to get permission for habitation.

If your property does not have an earth and/or tripswitch you are obliged by law 46/90 which came into action in March 1990 to have an electrician install them. According to this law all properties must have an earth and tripswitch installed by December 1994.

Plasterers

The *intonacatore* (plasterer) usually works on the same terms as builders and decorators (see above). The price you pay depends on the type of finish you require. Costs for various finishes, priced per square metre are approximately as follows:

rustic finish	28,000Lit.
smooth finish	35,000Lit.
skim coating	11,000Lit.
renovation of old plaster	9,200Lit.
filler	2,900Lit.

Plumbers

An *idraulico* (plumber) works for between 30,000 and 35,000Lit. per hour. If you are having a major installation such as central heating or a bathroom plumbed in, you will probably be quoted a price for the whole job. To have central heating installed in an apartment with an area of 100 square metres (ceiling height approximately 2.7 m), including the boiler, radiators, thermostat and piping, costs in the region of 6,000,000Lit; to have an ordinary bathroom installed with an area of about 6 square metres costs around 2,500,000Lit.

If a plumber is installing a complete central heating system you may wish to request an official certificate which can then be shown when it comes to selling your property (Fig. 29 is an example of such a certificate).

DICHIARAZIONE DI CONFORMITA' DELL'IMPIANTO ALLA REGOLA DELL'ARTE
(art. 18, legge n° 46 del 5 marzo 1990)

Il sottoscritto ①
titolare/legale rappresentante/direttore tecnico dell'impresa (ragione
sociale ②

operante nel settore ③

con sede in Via _____ n° _____ } ④

Comune _____ (prov. _____) tel. _____

P. IVA ⑤ iscritta nel Registro delle Ditte(R.D. 20.09.1934

n° 2011) di ⑥ n° ⑦ iscritta Albo Provinciale

Imprese Artigiane (L. 8.8.85 n° 443) di ⑧ n° ⑨

esecutrice dell'impianto(descrizione schematica) ⑩

_____

_____

_____

_____

installato nei locali siti nel Comune di ⑪ (prov. ⑫)

Via ⑬ n° ⑭ scala _____ piano _____

interno _____ di proprietà di (nome, cognome, indirizzo _____

_____

adibito ad uso ___ industriale ___ civile ___ terziario ___ commercio ___ } ⑮
altri usi ___

D I C H I A R A

che l'opera è stata eseguita conformemente al progetto predisposto da(nome, } ⑯
cognome, indirizzo) ....
Tipo di lavoro eseguito:
___ modificato/ampliato ___ impianto nuovo ___ lavoro di manutenzione } ⑰

Allegati: a) Progetto:....................................

D E C L I N A

ogni responsabilità per sinistri a persone o a cose derivanti da manomissio-
ne dell'impianto da parte di terzi, ovvero da carenze di manutenzione o ri-
parazione o vetustà.   Data ⑱

IL COMMITTENTE   IL TITOLARE LEGALE RAPPRESENTANTE ⑲
_____

1. Name of person who carried out work
2. Name of company that carried out work
3. Type of work carried out
4. Address and telephone number
5. VAT number
6. Place where registered
7. Registration number
8. Place where inscribed on professional register
9. Professional register inscription number
10. Details of work carried out
11. Commune in which work was carried out
12. Province in which work was carried out
13. Street in which work was carried out
14. Street number at which work was carried out
15. Type of building in which work was carried out
16. Declaration that installation conformed to regulations
17. Nature of work carried out
18. Date
19. Signature

Fig. 29. Declaration for installation certificate

Tilers

Tiling is an art in Italy and there is a greater selection of tiles than any other form of floor covering. The *piastrellista* (tiler) will either lay tiles that you have already bought or will supply the tiles you request. You may find it is more economical to order the tiles through the tiler as he will probably get a builder's discount. To have some idea of the cost of having a floor tiled see the following chart. (Since there is such a large differential in price between different quality tiles a separate price is given for materials and labour. If you are endeavouring to tile a floor on the cheap you may wish to enquire about *seconda qualita* (second-quality) tiles, those that have slight defects. The prices below are for first-quality tiles and are per square metre.)

Type of tiles	*Material*	*Labour*
composite marble 20 x 20 cm	50,000Lit.	70,000Lit.
marble 30 x 30 x 1.5 cm:		
Bianco Carrara	76,000Lit.	60,000Lit.
Travertino Romano	50,000Lit.	60,000Lit.
Verde Alpi	220,000Lit.	60,000Lit.
ceramic 30 x 30 cm	25,000Lit.	40,000Lit.

Tilers tile walls as well as floors. To have a wall tiled with ceramic tiles, 20 x 20 cm in dimension, costs around 75,000Lit. per square metre inclusive of both labour and materials. To have the same type of tiles laid in a diagonal arrangement costs slightly more — around 85,000Lit. per square metre, inclusive of labour and materials.

Price catalogues for the building trade

If you are undertaking a really major project involving a lot of outgoings you may be interested in writing for the price catalogues for the building trade. There are twelve catalogues in total, each dedicated to a different branch of the building trade. The catalogues are not only a good source of finding out costs but also materials that are available, although of course it is all written in Italian. The address to contact for further information is as follows:

DEI Tipografia del Genio Civile
Via Nomentana 16
00161 Rome
Tel: (06) 4402046.

DOING IT YOURSELF

You may be one of those many people who dream of buying a cheap derelict property and renovating it yourself at your leisure. It is by no means impossible in Italy, but it is certainly more difficult and expensive than in the UK where there is much more in the way of DIY materials, tools and experience available.

DIY is not an Italian leisure-time activity. Most shudder at the thought of even putting up a picture hook. You will be regarded with respect and awe by your neighbours and friends as well as professionals in the building trade, but you will be quite on your own in your endeavours and will have none of the handy pre-packaged goods available in British DIY stores at your disposal, nor will you be able to hire some of the larger equipment necessary. You will have to muck along with professional builders and try to do things their way, using the materials they use.

The first place to locate in your nearest town is the *edilizia* (the builder's yard) which stocks everything from sacks of cement, sand and roof tiles to bathroom suites, plumbing parts and insulation. Your next most important source is the *ferramenta* (hardware store), which sells household paint, varnishes, tools, nails and often wood trims such as cornices and skirting boards.

With these two basic sources of materials in mind the following section lists what materials are generally available in Italy and how to say them in Italian, which is half your battle done. Information and relevant glossaries are arranged in subject groups and listed alphabetically.

Building and construction

The *edilizia* (builder's yard) is open five days a week and usually Saturday morning too. Sometimes the *edilizia* closes one weekday afternoon — this varies from place to place. Opening hours tend to be similar to those for businesses, usually from 8.30 am to 12.30 pm and 3–4 pm to 6–7 pm. Most builder's yards will deliver materials at an extra cost.

If you use a builder's yard regularly, once they get to know you, your purchases will be put on an account. When you take materials on account, that is without having received a till receipt, you should be given a **bolla di consegna** (delivery note) which can be presented to the finance police should you be stopped and asked to prove the validity of the goods.

It is general practice to go to a builder's yard with a clear idea of what you want rather than expecting to be able to browse around. Materials are usually stacked in inaccessible places, not on view to the public. The following is a list of vocabulary that you may find useful both at the builder's yard and the hardware store.

betoniera	cement mixer
blocchi	hollow clay building blocks
canna da fumo	chimney pipe
cartongesso	plasterboard
calce	lime
cazzuola	trowel
coppo	roof tile
cacciavite	screwdriver
cemento	cement
cemento bianco	white cement
chiodi	nails
condotto	duct
filo di ferro	metal wire
frattazzo	float
ganci	hooks
gesso	plaster
ghiaia	gravel
girabecchino	hand drill
isolamento	insulation
lana di vetro	mineral fibre
livello a bolle d'aria	spirit level
malta	smooth cement
martello	hammer
mattoni forati	hollow bricks
mattoni pieni	bricks
mattoni refrettari	refractory bricks
mazza	mallet
morsetto	clamp
pala	shovel
piale	plane
pinze	pincers
polistirene espanso	expansive polystyrene for insulation
polvere	crushed rock

sabbia	sand
scagliola intonaco	slow-setting plaster
sega	saw
seghetto per metalle	metal saw
spatola	spatula
squadra a battente	set square
tasselli	raw-plugs
tavelle	construction blocks
tenaglie	pincers
tondino	reinforcing metal wire
trapano elettrico	electric drill
travi di cemento armato	reinforced concrete beams
umidita di risalita	rising damp
viti	screws

Decoration

In Italy many households employ decorators rather than undertaking the general maintenance themselves. The market for decorating materials is therefore smaller than in the UK and consequently the selection too is more limited. Colour ranges are restricted, as are types of paint such as non-drip, and there is a very small, and also expensive, selection of wallpapers. The *ferramenta* (hardware store) will be the source of most of your materials but not your inspiration, although some *ferramenta* will mix colours to your requirements. The *ferramenta* keeps regular shop hours (8.30–12.30, 5–8), closing one afternoon in the week and also on Saturday afternoons and of course Sundays. The following vocabulary should be of help in getting together your shopping list and asking for the things in the shop itself. For vocabulary for tools and other implements that are also sold in a *ferramenta*, see the vocabulary list under 'building' (p. 103). Note also that among other things, the *ferramenta* usually cuts keys and sometimes glass.

acqua ragia	white spirit
carta da parati	wall paper
carta fodera	lining paper
carta lavabile	washable wallpaper
carta tipo vinilico	vinyl wallpaper
carta vetrata	sandpaper
chiodi	nails
colla	glue
filo a piombo	plumb line

forbici	scissors
idropittura	water resistant emulsion
intonacare	to plaster
nastro di carta adesiva	masking tape
pennello	paintbrush
penello ad angolo	radiator brush
penello piatto	flat paintbrush
penello rotondo	round paintbrush
piccone	pick
pittura lavabile	washable emulsion
pitture	paints
raschietto	flat stripping knife
revestimenti murale	wall coverings
rullino premigiunti	seam roller
rullo per verniciare	roller for painting
sega	saw
smalto	gloss paint
spazzola	brush
spazzola metallica	wire brush
spugna	sponge
stucco antico	textured paint
stucco gia pronto	ready-mixed filler
stucco in polvere	filler in powdered form
tampone	paint pad
tempera	non-washable emulsion
tende	blinds
vernice	varnish or gloss paint
vernice antiruggine	anti-rust paint
viti	screws

Electrics

If you are renovating a property that needs completely rewiring you will have to employ an authorised electrician who will supply the certificates and guarantees officially necessary in the event of future sale. The electrician oversees all electrical connections as far as the fuse box which is the property of ENEL (Ente Nazionale per l'Energia Elettrica). ENEL control the amount of electricity that is supplied, the maximum being 3 kw.

If you want a larger electricity supply than this, you must have another meter installed which of course incurs extra expense and rental charges. If you overload your electricity supply the tripswitch, now obligatory, will intervene. Before flicking the tripswitch back on remember to turn off one of the appliances that caused it to overload in the first place.

Minor jobs to do with electricity you may want to do yourself. You will find materials in a specialist shop, usually called *materiale elettrico*. If you are bringing electrical appliances from the UK, check that they will run on the Italian current, which is 220 volts AC/50 Hertz, and remember that you will need to put Italian plugs on, which are unfused and consist of either two pins or three pins in a single row.

The vocabulary below should help you when purchasing electrical goods and materials, for, as is invariably the case, you will have to ask for what you want at the counter rather than browse around and pick items off a shelf.

apriporta elettrico	electrically operated door
cacciavite	screwdriver
cavo	flex
condutore	conducting wire
connettore	connector
contatore	meter
filo	wire
fusibili	fuses
giunzione	junction
guaino	plastic covering on wire
illuminazione	lighting
interruttori	switches
interruttori automatici	tripswitches
lampadina	light bulb
morsetto	terminal grip
morsetto fermacavo	cord grip
nastro isolante	insulating tape
pinze da elettricista	pliers
pinze spellafili	wire-stripping pincers
presa	socket
presa incassata	recessed socket
scatola	box
spina	plug
termostato	thermostat
terra	earth
tubo di protezione	plastic chanelling
tubo flesibile	flexible chanelling
tubo rigido	rigid chanelling

Flooring

In the eyes of Italians, flooring, in whatever form, is most definitely a job
for the professional. However, if you wish to have a go on your own, read
on. Tiles of all shapes, colours and sizes, terracotta to high-glazed, are
sold at the *edilizia*, builder's yard, or at one of the many prestigious stores
that sell kitchens and bathrooms.

You will find an enormous selection in the form of display cards,
although only a few will actually be in stock, most only being available
on order. If you are ordering a style that is not in stock, follow up the initial
request regularly to check that they have been able to get them and that
the tile you have chosen has not been discontinued. Promises of arrival a
week later are not always realistic; it is better to place your order at least
a month or so before you actually require them.

Perhaps the next most popular type of flooring is parquet, but unless
you already have experience you will be undoubtedly employing someone
to lay it. It is generally sold in stores that specialise in parquet and have a
very wide selection to choose from at a very wide range of prices. The
prices depend not only on the type of wood and the dimension, but the
quality of the grain. *Prima scelta* (first quality) has a completely regular
grain; *seconda scelta* (second quality) has occasional knots, while *scarto*
(rejects) are irregular in size, grain and texture.

Unfortunately, the expense of parquet is not only in the actual wood,
but also the glue with which to fix it (particularly if you need the strong
glue for larger dimension parquet) and the sealant and polish. Prices per
square metre for first-quality parquet are as follows (you can expect to
pay from half to two-thirds of these prices for second-quality):

6–8 cm wide, 14–17 mm thick	70–120,000Lit.
4–6 cm wide, 9–11 mm thick	50–100,000Lit.
mosaic squares, 8 mm thick	30–42,000Lit.

Wall-to-wall carpet is not a very popular option as a floor covering in
Italy. It is generally sold at pricy interior design type shops that also make
blinds and curtains to measure. For a polyester carpet you can expect to
pay around 40,000Lit. per square metre and almost double that for one
made of wool. Rush-matting is the same price as a polyester carpet. The
shop that sells the carpet will also arrange for a fitter to lay it.

Linoleum is also less common in Italy than it is in the UK. The
ferramenta often stocks a limited selection, at quite reasonable prices, but
if you are looking for cushion-backed lino or something with style you
will have to try a carpet shop.

The following is a list of vocabulary that may be of use when you are selecting a floor covering.

ceramica	ceramic tiles
colla	glue
cotto	terracotta
feltro	felt underlay
formato	size/shape
juta naturale	natural backing
juta sintetica	synthetic backing
gomma	vinyl
inchiodata	tacked
lana	wool
largezza	width
linoleum	linoleum
lunghezza	length
malta di sigilla	grout
marmo	marble
moquette	carpet
parquet	parquet
pavimento	floor
posa	laying
rotoli	roll
spessore	thickness
superficie satinata	matt surface
superficie lucida	gloss surface
supporto schiuma	sponge backing

Plumbing

For plumbing materials your best bet is to go to the *edilizia* (building yard) although for materials related to heating systems go to the shop that initially sold the boiler or other parts of the system. There are three basic systems used for supply plumbing: plastic, iron and copper, in that order of preference. Copper plumbing is predominantly used with brass pressure joints, although soldering is used in some circumstances. Waste plumbing is done in plastic and in concrete, there being two grades of the plastic tubing, white and orange; the orange is thicker, more durable and also more expensive.

The following vocabulary list should help you in asking for what you need.

box doccia	shower unit
caldaia murale	wall boiler
dado	bolt
fascette	bracket
filettatura	plumbing tape
guarnizione	washer
lavabo	wash-basin
lavello	sink
liquido sgrassante	flux
manicotto	sleeve
piatto doccia	shower base
raccordo	joint
radiatori	radiators
riscaldamento	heating
rubinetto	tap
saldatura	soldering
sifone	U-bend
stagno	solder
tubi di plastica	plastic pipes
tubi di rami	copper pipes
tubi di scarico	wastepipes
tubi zincati	zinc-coated iron pipes
valvola	valve
vasca di bagno	bath tub
vaso igienico	toilet

Woodwork

Woodwork is expensive in Italy, the price of wood being generally higher than in the UK. As much of the wood is imported, prices vary according to the vagaries of the exchange markets. To buy wood you must locate your nearest *legnami* (timber yard). There are generally two types, those that sell *legname da costruzione* (timber for construction) and those that sell *legname da lavoro* (timber to be worked). Timber yards are generally open five days a week and closed at the weekends. They tend to keep office hours, that is having a shorter lunch break than do the shops (8.30–12.30, 2.30–6). For nails, screws and all tools, go to your local *ferramenta* (hardware store).

The following is a vocabulary list that may come in handy when you are buying materials for a woodworking project. Some of the more general tools that you may use are listed under 'building' (see above, p. 103).

abete	fir/deal
bedano	beveller
blochetto per levigare	sanding block
bullone	bolt
cacciavite	screwdriver
cacciavite con punta stella	philips screwdriver
carta vetrata	sandpaper
grana media/fine	medium/fine grain
castagna	chestnut
cera	wax
cerniere	hinge
chiodi	nails
chiodi di calzolaio	tacks
chiodi di ottone	brass nails
chiave	spanner
colla vinilica per legno	wood glue
compensato	composite board
ganci	hooks
girabecchino	hand drill
impregnate	preservative
lacche poliuretaniche	polyurethane
lama di seghetto	saw blade
legno	wood
levigatrice orbitale	orbital sander
levatrice a nastro	belt sander
levigatura	sanding
listelli	small planks or strips
lucidate	varnished
maniglia	handle
martello	hammer
matita di falegname	carpentry pencil
modanatura	moulding
metro a nastro	tape measure
morsetto serragiunti	clamp
pasta di legno	wood-filler
piallate	planed
piallone	plane
pino	pine
pomelli	knobs
punta	drill bit
quercia	oak

raspa	file
saracco	wood saw
scalpello da legno	wood chisel
sega	saw
sega circolare	band saw
seghetto alternativo	jig saw
serratura	lock
serrature magnetiche	magnetic catches

5
Moving In

MOVING

As both Italy and the UK are members of the EC, moving house to Italy should be no different from moving house within the UK. In reality, moving from the UK to Italy involves a good deal more organisation. There are not only odds and ends to tie up before you leave, but there is also the preparation of paperwork for your arrival in Italy and of course the language barrier. This chapter deals with how to organise your move, getting ready and what you should do on arrival in bureaucratic terms.

Removal companies

The best way of moving furniture and belongings from Britain to Italy is to use an international removal firm. Be sure to use a firm that undertakes all the necessary paperwork, preferably including the compilation of the inventory, which must be written in English and Italian. Most removal firms also take charge of the packing and unpacking. It is worth checking just how a company packages: for example, the best firms use two outer layers of waterproof wrapping with four cushioning layers inside.

You should also check on the insurance conditions. A basic premium is usually around $1\frac{1}{2}$–2 per cent with an increased premium for valuable objects that amount to over 20 per cent of the total amount insured. As a precaution, whether the removal company are making the inventory or not, you should make your own comprehensive list of everything that is being packed so that you can claim for anything that is lost or broken in carriage.

The amount charged by the removal company is generally calculated by volume. If your belongings fill an entire container you could be paying in the region of £2,500. The most cost effective way is to share a container. All companies routinely offer this service, although it can mean waiting around, particularly if you are moving to an unpopular spot such as remote southern Italy. There is less waiting in the summer when removals are more frequent, and northern Italy, especially Tuscany, are the most popular destinations.

The best place to look for a removal company is in your local Yellow Pages. It is worth asking around for estimates first; most companies offer quotations without obligation. Remember that your quotation may be exclusive of VAT which is presently at $17^1/2$ per cent.

The addresses of the head office of some major international removal companies are as follows.

Allied Pickfords
Riverside House
Stonehill Business Park
Angel Road
London N18 3LD
Tel: (081) 807 2223.

Britannia
Serin House
Hindsley Place
London SE23 2NF
Freephone: 0800 212024.

Scotpac
Kingsbridge Road
Barking
Essex
Tel: (081) 591 3388.

Trans Euro
Drury Way
Brent Park
London NW10 0JN
Tel: (081) 784 0100.

Interpack Worldwide Ltd
Unit 11, Hanover West Trading Estate
161 Acton Lane
London NW10
Tel: (081) 965 5550.

AGS International
2 Bush Industrial Estate
Standard Road
London NW10 6DF
Tel: (081) 961 7595.

If you are not using a removal firm, but transporting belongings under your own steam, you should have no major difficulties since the lifting of the border regulations within the EC. However, if you are bringing furniture from Britain which is over fifty years old you should apply for permission from the Italian Ministry of Culture beforehand and then declare it on arrival to avoid difficulties in re-exporting it. The address for the Italian Ministry of Culture is as follows:

Ministero Beni Culturali
Ufficio Esportazione Oggetti d'Arte
Via Cernaia 1
Roma
Tel: (06) 4881457.

What to pack
Having considered the transportation of your goods and belongings, you should next think about packing. Planning to buy new when you get to Italy may be an expensive option. You may also find that what you were planning to buy is not available. If you have read the chapter on house renovation you will be well aware of the scarcity of DIY materials and therefore may wish to take a supply with you.

You should also consider taking flat-pack units, especially if you are installing a kitchen, for although Italian kitchens are attractive, they are very pricy: once an Italian has invested in one, when they move house they take their kitchen with them. Furniture is also much more expensive in Italy, there being no mega chain stores offering cut-price discounts, or cheap secondhand furniture shops. Furniture that is regarded as junk or bric-à-brac in the UK is given antique status in Italy and priced accordingly.

Fitted carpets, should you want them, are also worth bringing from the UK, both for the competitiveness in price and quality. Bedding in Italy is beautiful and you can pick up fine, embroidered sheets at local markets as well as very well-made and prettily coloured eiderdowns. However, duvets are not very widely used and cost at least double their UK price — so if you have one, pack it.

As far as electrical appliances go, although they are slightly more expensive, you are probably better off buying them in Italy where they are adapted to run on 220 V and covered by local guarantee. An electric kettle, however, is well worth bringing as the Italians are not a tea-drinking nation and have no use for them; hence they are scarce and very expensive. If you do pack electrical appliances then try to bring the sales invoice in case you need to prove that you have paid VAT, although you may still have to pay the difference of $1^1/_2$ per cent between Italian VAT and British.

You should note that British TV sets and portable phones tend not to function properly on the Italian system. Other incompatible appliances are lamps or light fittings which take bayonet bulbs as only the screw-in type are used in Italy. Plugs are different too, so if you are bringing an appliance with a built-in plug you will need an adaptor.

Unless you enjoy lavishing money on stylish clothes, pack as large a wardrobe as possible. Apart from outdoor markets, cut-price clothing is just not Italian. *Saldi* (sales) take place in January and early February, and also in late July and August before summer vacation begins, but even then you will pay above the odds.

Remember that winter is as cold in Italy as it is in the UK, so include a raincoat and a winter coat if you are planning being in Italy then. If you have a fur coat this may be your chance to wear it. Animal rights campaigners are neither active nor militant in Italy and Italians love wearing fur. Sportswear and sports equipment are also something you should consider bringing with you if you wish to save money.

If you are moving to Italy with your children then, for purposes of economy, make sure they have a good supply of clothing packed too. There is no Italian equivalent to Mothercare, Boots, Early Learning or any of the other reasonably priced chain stores that exist in Britain. Benetton, Prenatal and Chicco are the principal Italian chains, but they are not cheap. If you are travelling with a baby you may wish to pack a supply of favourite foods as the selection is somewhat restricted in Italy, and the Italian diet is very different to the British.

It is a good idea to pack a few of your own favourite foods too as Italians eat Italian and nothing else, so that ingredients for other cuisines are not widely available. Spices and condiments are particularly useful to bring. Cooking utensils are also somewhat different in Italy, and while you will be able to buy superb saucepans and colanders for pasta, you will not find woks or traditional British saucepans with lids and a single handle very commonplace.

If you still have space in your packing, slip in a box or two of tea as it not only makes good gifts but is much more expensive to buy in Italy. Italian tea brands include Winston and Yellow Label, with tea of every flavour from apple to cherry, but you will find little in the way of bulk household tea. Indeed, bulk household anything apart from wine, pasta and washing powder is not common. This includes toiletry products which are sold in expensive pharmacies or small boutiques rather than in mass production as on the shelves of Boots and the like. Body Shop have opened up chains in the major cities. Generally, however, toiletries, cosmetics and pharmaceuticals are cheaper from the UK.

If you take a regular prescribed drug, pack a good supply to give you time to locate its equivalent in Italy. Many drugs are marketed under different names. Your UK doctor or the drug manufacturer should be able to tell you the brand name used in Italy, and whether the formula given in Italy is exactly the same as your current prescription.

Moving your pets

To bring a domestic animal into Italy you will have to have a health check administered by an official vet at the border and you must also present the following two documents:

- Export Health Certificate;
- Rabies Certificate.

To obtain an Export Health Certificate, the first step is to request application form EXA1 from the Ministry of Agriculture, Fisheries and Food at the following address:

Ministry of Agriculture, Fisheries and Food
Government Buildings (Toby Jug Site)
Hook Rise South
Tolworth
Surbiton
Surrey KT6 7NF
Tel: (081) 330 4411.

Application form EXA1 should then be filled in and sent to your local Animal Health Office. The certificate will next be passed to an approved local veterinary inspector. The vet will examine your animal within 48 hours of your departure and issue you with the completed export certificate.

The local veterinary inspector will also issue a Rabies Certificate. A rabies vaccine must be given not less than 20 days and not more than 11 months before leaving the UK. The rabies vaccine is not obligatory for animals under three months of age, or those that are being transported unaccompanied. If you are travelling through other places on the way to Italy, apply to the authorities in the relevant countries for their stipulations.

LOCAL BUREAUCRACY

Once you arrive in Italy you will have various bureaucratic formalities to fulfil in order to obtain all the right pieces of paper that are needed in day-to-day transactions. This section outlines what is needed and how to go about getting them.

Registering

One of your first brushes with bureaucracy should take place within three days of arriving in Italy. Go to the local **Questura**, or **Commissariato** or **Stazione di Carabinieri** (the police station) to register yourself. Should you be staying in a hotel or other holiday accommodation you don't need to worry as you will be automatically registered.

Permits

If you are staying in Italy for more than 30 days you need to apply for a **Permesso di Soggiorno** (Permit to Stay) at the **Ufficio Stranieri** (Foreign Department) in the police headquarters of your regional capital. If your regional capital is not easily accessible you may find your local police willing to apply for the permit on your behalf, in which case you will have to write a formal letter of request accompanied by a *bollo* (state stamp).

Fig. 30 is an example letter of request. It should be typed on the official paper sold at *tabacchi* by the sheet, known as *carta uso bollo*. Fix the *bollo* in the right hand of the two wide margins that are drawn at either side.

Members of EC countries are given special permits entitled **Carta di Soggiorno di Cittadino di Uno Stato Membro della CEE** which are valid for up to five years. Non-EC members are issued with a **Documento di Soggiorno** which is usually only valid for one or two years. The procedure is to complete the application form, and return it to the police with the following documents:

- passport;
- photocopy of principal pages of passport;
- 3 passport-sized photographs;
- health insurance or Form E111;
- *bollo* (state stamp).

Alla Questura di [insert province]
[your name]

Il sottoscritto, anato/a [place of birth]
il [date of birth] *cittadino/a* [nationality]
in possesso di passaporto n. [passport number]
rilasciato il [date of issue] *e valido fino al* [expiry date] *rivolge corte domanda affinché gli/le venga l'autorizzazione per soggionare in Italia,* [place], *per motivi di studio/lavoro/salute* [delete as applicable].

Allega:
[make a list of enclosures]
Il/la richiedente ha fatto ingresso in Italia il [date of entry into Italy] *tramite la frontiera di* [name of frontier crossed].
Recapito all'estero: [date of return]
Inoltre, dichiara di abitare a [Italian address].

Con osservanza
Firma [legible signature]

Fig. 30. Application for a Permit to Stay.

You may also be asked to present evidence of being able to maintain yourself, which means either a letter from an employer or a letter from your bank stating your private means. Once you have met these conditions, and possibly others such as evidence of health insurance, your permit will be ready within a month or so.

Residency

To be a resident in Italy you must have a **Permesso di Soggiorno**, passport or identity card and a permanent local address. Provided you meet these requirements registration is a straightforward process carried out at the **ufficio anagrafe** (municipal registry office) which is usually located within the local *comune* or *municipo* (town hall). You will need to return to this office each time you require a **Certificato di Residenza**, (Residence Certificate), a document that is required in most domestic transactions from having electricity connected to opening a bank account. Sometimes you may need to attach the requisite *bollo* to the certificate, which is always a costly business, although the charge for the certificate itself is nominal.

Italian tax code number

The Italian tax code number, **Codice Fiscale**, is an obligatory document for anyone resident in Italy, regardless of age; even new-born babies have them. It is a document that is often demanded for the most trivial transactions from buying a fridge to joining a local evening class. To obtain a *Codice Fiscale* locate the *Ufficio Imposte Dirette* (your provincial tax office), and present your passport or identity card. A card with your tax number on it will be issued on the spot and should be carried on you at all times.

Driving licence

Resident foreigners in Italy are only allowed to drive on a non-Italian driving licence for one year from the date on which they registered their residency. One solution to this is to buy an international driver's licence (only available outside Italy) which must be renewed annually. Otherwise you are obliged to go through a very lengthy procedure to obtain an Italian driving licence. If you need help, go to any local *agenzia* that advertises licences *(patente)* in their window or to an ACI (Automobile Club Italiano) office. In the final stages you are bound to employ the services of an *agenzia* or ACI office.

There is a certain amount, however, that you can do yourself. The first step is to make a translation of your existing licence. If you have a

Dipartimento di trasporto [inset country]

Patente di guida, tipo [insert type]

Nome: [insert first names]

Cognome: [insert surname]

Date e luogo di Nascita: [insert place and date of birth]

Domicilio: [insert address]

Rilasciato dal: [insert issuing office]

Il giorno: [insert date of issue]

Valido fino al [insert expiry date]

Patente [insert licence number]

Autorizzata a guidare tipo [insert code for type of vehicles authorised to drive] *soltanto i moto veicoli tipo* [insert code for authorised vehicles] *se il conducente ha l' eta per guidare. Vedere il regolamento minimo eta per guidare che e nella parte posteriore. A 18 anni: Motoveicoli con il massimo portata di peso non superiore a 7.5 Ton. Altri moto veicoli autorizzati di merce. Grande veicolo per passegeri in concomitanza con la regola No. 4 del motoveicoli [Licenza di guida]. Regolamenti 1987. Vedere trasporto merce pesante e veicoli di trasporto pubblico. A 21 anni: Motoveicoli grandi per passegeri, con il massimo peso piu di 7.5 Ton. Altri veicoli non elencati sopra. Vedere Guida di merce pesante e Veicoli di Servizio Pubblico.*

Fig. 31. Translation of driving licence.

I summenzionati limiti di eta non saranno applicati per i veicoli del gruppo A, B, G, H, K, L e N quando sono per uso Navale Militare ossia per motivi di Forze Aero.

Per guidare veicolo per merce pesante e Veicoli di Servizio Pubblico: Devi ottenere una licenza supplementare prima di guidare sia un veicolo pesante o veicolo de servizio pubblico.

Veicolo grande per passegeri, si intende un veicolo a positamente costruito ossia trasportare piu di 9 persone compreso il conducente.

Veicoli per merce: si intende un veicolo, eccetto moto veicolo grande per passegeri o pure trattori per agricoltura, costruito o adattato per trasportare tirare e con il massimo peso ecedente 3.5 Ton. Il massimo peso e il peso massimo quando il veicolo potrebbe pesare a pieno carico comprende il peso de qualunque rimorchio o semi rimorchio. Elenco di tipo di licenze per guidare:

A. Qualunque veicoli eccetto veicoli gruppo D (Moto veicoli), tipo E (Ciclomotore), tipo G (rullo compressore), tipo H (cingolato caterpillar), tipo J (veicoli per invalidi)

E. Ciclomotore di 50CC

La sudetta patente porta un numero ad ogni margine [insert code numbers printed on edges of licence].

Fig. 31. Continued.

European-Community-type British driving licence you will be able to use the sample translation (see Fig. 31). The translation should be typed out on to the official *carta uso bollo*, which is available from *tabacchi* (tobacconists), and a *bollo* (state stamp) should be affixed in the right hand of the two wide margins. Once the translation is written, take it to be stamped and signed at your local *pretura* or *tribunale* (magistrate's court).

The next stage in the procedure is to buy a *bollo* at the *tabacchi* and have it officially stamped on to a *Certificato di Residenza* by the *ufficio anagrafe* in your local *comune* or *municipio*. At the same time take along three passport-sized photographs of yourself and ask someone to authenticate one of them, verifying that it is a true likeness.

Next you must pick up the appropriate forms for a **Certificato Medico** (medical certificate) at your local Unita Sanitaria Locale (USL). Take the forms to your family doctor to have a report filled in and signed. Then return to USL, where you should have an eye test, and hand over the following:

- doctor's report;
- a *bollo* (state stamp);
- 1 passport-sized photograph.

Having completed all this and anything else USL might request, you should be issued with a medical certificate.

From this point on you could employ an *agenzia* or someone who works in ACI (Automobile Club Italiano) to take each of the documents you have compiled as well as your current driving licence to the **Motorizzazione** office. The following is a checklist of the documents you will need.

- stamped and signed licence translation;
- original driving licence;
- stamped residence certificate;
- 3 passport-sized photographs (one endorsed);
- stamped medical certificate.

If you prefer to go yourself you can find the address of the *Motorizzazione* office by looking in the Yellow Pages under *Ministero del Trasporto*. Be warned however that *Motorizzazione* have a reputation for being unhelpful, especially towards foreigners. Once you are in the hands of *Motorizzazione* anything can happen, and one often has the suspicion that a bribe would help smooth out the difficulties. Resist and try to keep your patience and find just that one more bit of official paper, that extra *bollo* or two, and a postal order payment.

There will probably be a period during which you will have neither your original driving licence nor your new Italian driving licence. If this situation should arise get a photocopy made of your original licence and ask for a cover letter from the official to whom you handed over your documents.

Once you are in possession of an Italian driving licence you will be liable to pay licence tax. Known as **marche per patente** (state stamp for licences), one must be affixed in the back of your licence every year. They are sold at the post office and also in most *tabacchi* (tobacconists). The cost goes up every year. In 1991 it was Lit.22,000 and in 1993 it was increased to Lit.50,000. Italian driving licences are only valid for two years, after which an eye test must be completed before a new one is issued (see Fig. 32 for a facsimile of an Italian driving licence, page 124).

BASIC SERVICES

Moving into a new home will most probably require having various services connected (*allacciato*), namely gas, electricity and telephone. This section deals with each of the basic services, describing the procedures involved, from getting connected to paying bills. You should keep receipts of all bills paid and also the official declarations that are given for any installations or modifications that are made. Information is also provided as to the different heating options available so that you can best decide how to heat your home during the winter.

Electricity

ENEL (Ente Nazionale per l'Energia Elettrica) is the national electricity board, although there are also private companies now in operation particularly within the industrial sector in northern Italy where hydroelectric power is available. Domestic supply, however,is generally dealt with by ENEL who oversee the following:

- bringing the electricity supply to a property;
- the installation, connection and reading of meters;
- increasing or decreasing the power supply.

To find the local head office, look under ENEL in your local telephone directory, but if you are having electricity connected you will need to go

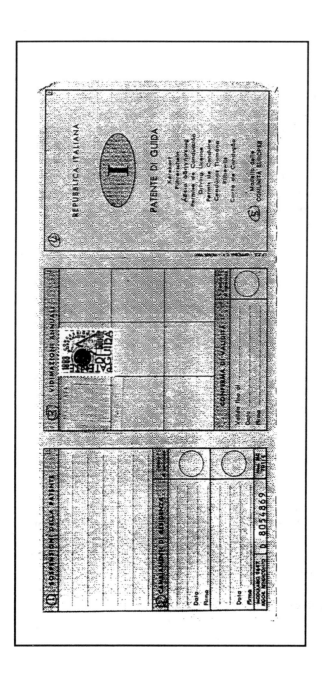

1. Suspension
2. Change of address
3. Annual authentication - official stamp to be affixed each year
4. Front cover
5. European Community model

Fig. 32. An Italian driving licence: *(above)* front; *(right)* back.

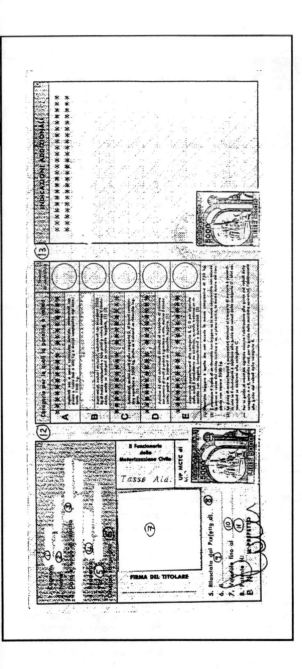

1. Surname
2. Name
3. Date and place of birth
4. Place of residency
5. Street
6. Blood group
7. Photo of driver
8. Issuing office
9. Date of issue
10. Validity date
11. Licence number
12. Categories for which licence is valid
13. Additional points

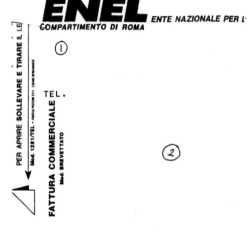

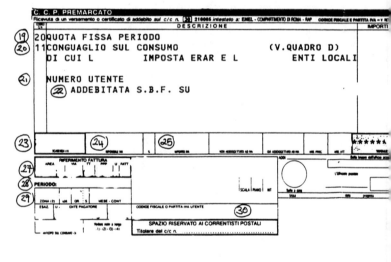

1. Issuing office
2. Your name and address
3. Bill reference number
4. Period to which bill applies
5. ENEL reference code
6. Type of electricity supply
7. Maximum electricity power supply
8. Period being re-assessed
9. Last meter reading
10. Previous meter reading

11. Total consumption
12. Breakdown of estimated and actual consumption bi-monthly
13. Difference between estimated and actual consumption in total
14. Amount due in difference between estimated and actual consumption
15. Information regarding phoning in your meter readings

Fig. 33. Electricity bill.

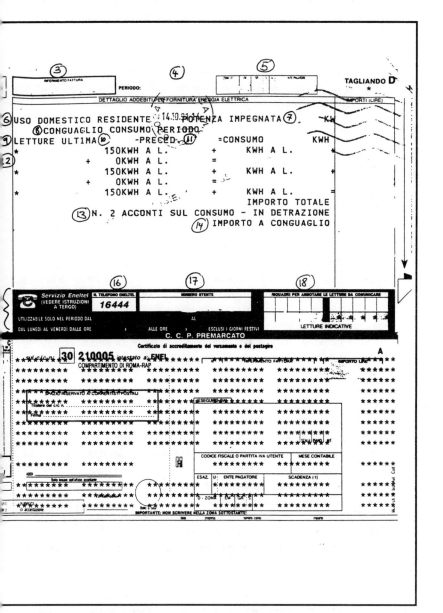

to the office itself to open a contract. First telephone to find out their opening hours (they are invariably closed in the afternoon) and also the documents you will need to take, although generally the following are required:

- passport or identity card;
- *codice fiscale*;
- *certificato di residenza*;
- last meter reading.

The contract, among other things will state the amount of power at your disposal and whether you are resident or not. Note that non-residents pay considerably higher rates. Within a short time an ENEL employee will come to your home to do the necessary work. Once the meter is turning there is nothing more to do than wait for your first bill.

Bills are issued every two months and are calculated according to an estimated consumption rather than an actual one. Your bill will also include standing charges, tax and costs for any work you have done by ENEL. A bill based on your real consumption, known as a *conguaglio* is issued twice yearly (see Fig. 33 for a facsimile of ENEL bill). Should you be in credit you will receive the difference through the post in the form of a postal order which can be cashed at the post office.

Bills must be paid, within the stated date through a post office or bank where you will pay a small surcharge. If you are a resident in Italy you can arrange to have your electricity bills directly debited from a bank account. If you are not a resident, you should arrange for a neighbour to call in to pick up your bills, or have the bills addressed to someone who is willing to pay them on your behalf.

Gas

If your home in Italy is in an urban area you will most probably be connected to or have access to **metano citta** (town gas). If you want to be connected to *metano* the first step is to locate your local office by looking in the *Pagine Gialle* (Yellow Pages) under Gas Esercizio. Telephone the office, find out their opening hours and also the documents needed in order to be connected. Normal documents required are:

- *stato di famiglia*
- *certificato di residenza*
- *dichiarazione sostitutiva dell' atto notorieta*
- *codice fiscale*

RICHIESTA ESECUZIONE LAVORI E/O FORNITURA GAS

Codice Impianto ①

zona	utenza
②	③

codice via

④

Cognome   Nome

⑤

Via   Numero civico

Data, 21/10/1992

Scala   piano   interno

C.A.P.   Comune   Sigla Prov.

Cod. Fisc. Utente ⑥

Cod. Aliquota IVA

Alla Spett.le _____

Impianto di _____

In relazione alla domanda presentata ed al «regolamento di fornitura di gas agli utenti» in vigore, il sottoscritto si impegna a pagare le sottospecificate somme che saranno addebitate in fattura.

Contributo allacciamento
e fornitura   L. ⑨

Modifica allacc. e/o spostam.
contatore   L. ⑩

Contributo posa e/o apertura
contatore - subentro   L. ⑪

Anticipo fornitura   L. ⑫

Altre prestazioni   L. ⑬

IMPORTO TOTALE	L. ⑭	+ IVA

L'anticipo fornitura verrà restituito o conguagliato con la bolletta di ultima emissione, dedotto l'importo di eventuali forniture non pagate.

Tipo stabile
Codice utilizzo o merceologico
Codice tariffa
Codice statistico
Codice quota fissa
Codice calibro misuratore

Il Richiedente per accettazione

⑮

Copia per richiedente

1. Installation code
2. Zone
3. Consumer
4. Name
5. Address
6. Tax code number
7. Name of gas company
8. Town in which installation is made
9. Amount payable for connection and supply
10. Amount payable for modification to connection and/or changing position of meter
11. Amount payable for placing and/or re-opening meter
12. Forward payment for supply
13. Other services
14. Total amount payable plus VAT
15. Signature of client

Fig. 34. Gas supply and connection bill.

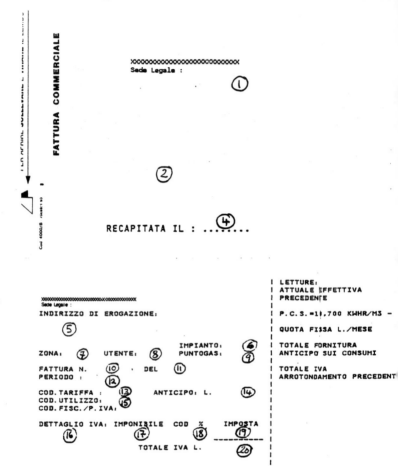

Sede Legale :

①

②

RECAPITATA IL : ...④...

LETTURE:
ATTUALE EFFETTIVA
PRECEDENTE

P.C.S. =1,700 KWHR/M3 –

QUOTA FISSA L./MESE

Sede Legale :
INDIRIZZO DI EROGAZIONE:

⑤

TOTALE FORNITURA
ANTICIPO SUI CONSUMI

IMPIANTO: ⑥
ZONA: ⑦   UTENTE: ⑧   PUNTOGAS: ⑨

FATTURA N. ⑩ . DEL ⑪
PERIODO :   ⑫

TOTALE IVA
ARROTONDAMENTO PRECEDENT

COD.TARIFFA : ⑬   ANTICIPO: L.   ⑭
COD.UTILIZZO: ⑮
COD.FISC./P.IVA:

DETTAGLIO IVA: IMPONIBILE COD %   IMPOSTA
               ⑯   ⑰   ⑱   ⑲
                        TOTALE IVA L.   ⑳

PROVV.CIP.   . CIRC. SNAM   ED EVENT.
CONGUAGLI   TOTALE FATTURA >> SALVO
ATTENZIONE: PER FACILI"

1. Issuing office
2. Your name and address
3. Advice and notices for customers
4. Date of delivery
5. Supply address
6. Installation number
7. Zone
8. Consumer number
9. Gas point number
10. Bill number
11. Date from which bill is valid
12. Months for which bill is valid
13. Tariff code
14. Forward payment
15. Usage code
16. VAT details
17. Taxable amount
18. Percentage of VAT

Fig. 35. Gas bill

NORME PER LA SICUREZZA DEGLI IMPIANTI
LA LEGGE 5 MARZO 1990 N. 46 " NORME PER LA SICUREZZA DEGLI
IMPIANTI " STABILISCE ALCUNI OBBLIGHI PER GLI UTENTI GAS :
- ESECUZIONE, MODIFICHE O AMPLIAMENTI DI IMPIANTI GAS DEVONO
  ESSERE AFFIDATI SOLAMENTE AD INSTALLATORI ABILITATI;
- L'UTENTE DEVE RICHIEDERE ALL'INSTALLATORE, A FINE LAVORI,
  UNA DICHIARAZIONE DI CONFORMITA' DELL'IMPIANTO ESEGUITO
  ALLE NORME DI LEGGE;
- GLI IMPIANTI GAS ESISTENTI , SE NON IN REGOLA , DEVONO
  ESSERE ADEGUATI ALLE NORME DI LEGGE.
PER ULTERIORI INFORMAZIONI RIVOLGERSI AGLI UFFICI METANO
CITTA' DI ZONA.

INOLTRE COMUNICHIAMO CHE, IN APPLICAZIONE DEL PROVVEDIMENTO
C.I.P. N. 25/91, CON DECORRENZA 01/03/93, LE TARIFFE PER
RISCALDAMENTO INDIVIDUALE CON O SENZA USO PROMISCUO E PER
ALTRI USI, ESCLUSE LE TARIFFE PER USO DOMESTICO (COTTURA
CIBI E ACQUA CALDA), AUMENTANO DI LIRE 7,1 AL METRO CUBO.

SI COMUNICA CHE, SUL B.U.R. DEL 18.1.93 E' STATA PUBBLICATA
LA LEGGE REGIONALE 14.1.93 NR.2 ART.2 CHE MODIFICA, CON
DECORRENZA 2.2.93 , LE IMPOSTE REGIONALI SUL GAS METANO
DA LIRE 10 A LIRE 30 AL METRO CUBO.

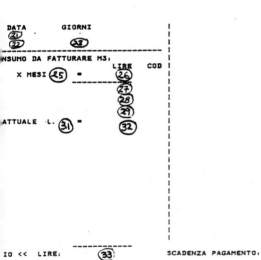

OPERAZIONI STRAPPARE LUNGO LA LINEA TRATTEGGIATA

19. Amount due
20. Total amount of VAT
21. Date of actual reading
22. Date of previous reading
23. Number of days between two readings
24. Fixed charge per month
25. Number of months
26. Total fixed charge for relevant number of months
27. Total amount for supply
28. Forward payment
29. Total VAT
30. Previous rounding-up of figures
31. Actual rounding-up of figures
32. Total amount from rounding-up of above figures
33. Total bill
34. Pay by date

All these documents with the exception of your *codice fiscale* (tax code number) are available from the *ufficio anagrafe* at your local *comune* or *municipio* (town hall). The third document in the above list is a standardised declaration of your good character.

With these documents in hand, go to the *metano citta* office and complete the appropriate forms. The two basic forms are:

- *richiesta esecuzione lavori e/o fornitura gas* (request to have work done and/or gas supplied);
- *domanda di fornitura e/o allaciamento* (demand for supply and/or connection)

Fig. 34 is a typical bill for having gas supplied and connected (p. 129).

Once your meter is turning, the next formality is to pay your bill. A *metano citta* employee will deliver your *fattura* (bill) every two months. Like electricity, the bill is calculated according to an estimated consumption rather than an actual consumption, with a *conguaglio* (reckoning-up bill) every six months. Also like electricity you will pay a standing charge and tax on each bill (see Fig. 35 for an example of a gas bill, page 130).

To pay your gas bill either go to a *metano citta* office where no charge is made, or go to a bank or post office where a small surcharge is added. If you are resident and have a bank account you can arrange for a direct debit. If you are not resident and do not visit your Italian home regularly then you should arrange for a neighbour to pay your bills.

Telephone

If you want to install or connect a telephone you will need to contact the national telephone company SIP (Societa Italiana per l'Esercizio delle Telecomunicazioni). This can be done over the phone by dialling the number 182 and requesting whichever of the three services below that you require:

- *trasloco* (moving);
- *subentro* (taking over a telephone);
- *nuovo impianto* (new installation).

In addition to your request, you will have to supply your name and address. Your request will probably be followed up by an acknowledgment through the post which will tell you the date by which the work should be carried out and also give you a reference number that should be kept for further communications.

If you are having a new telephone installed, a SIP technician will come to your home; however, the connection may not be made until a week or so later. The connection and other services are made by telephone communication which means that SIP will call you when the work is completed and supply new clients with their telephone number.

When your phone is connected the dialling tone will sound *('tu-tuuu')*; when you dial a number you will hear a ringing sound *('tuuu')* repeated at intervals. The continuous sound *('tu-tu-tu')* means the number is engaged. The charges made for using the telephone depend on the time of day and the distance. The categorisation of distance is as follows:

- Inter-urban
- Up to 15 km
- From 15 km to 30 km
- From 30 km to 60 km
- From 60 km to 120 km
- Over 120 km

The tariffs for the times of the day are organised as follows:

Peak hour	Monday–Friday, 8.30 am –1 pm	150%
Ordinary	Monday–Friday, 8–8.30 am, 1–6.30 pm	100%
	Saturday, 8 am–1 pm	100%
Reduced	Monday–Friday, 6.30–10 pm	70%
	Saturday, 1–10 pm	70%
	Sunday and public holidays, 8 am –10 pm	70%
Economy	Daily, 10 pm–8 am	50%

Telephone bills are sent every two months and are calculated on the number of **scatti** (meter points) you consume. You will also pay a regular rental charge and tax. It is possible to request a **documentazione traffico teleselettivo** (itemised bill) for which you will pay an additional charge of 35Lit. per item. Should you want such a bill, go to a local SIP office to make the request. The SIP office is also where you should pay your bills, although they can also be paid, at a small surcharge, at either the post office or bank. If you are not in Italy when your bills are due, arrange for someone to pay for them on your behalf. See Fig. 36 for a facsimile of a telephone bill (pages 134-135).

SIP
Società Italiana per l'Esercizio
delle Telecomunicazioni p.a.

①

FATTURA COMMERCIALE

SPEDIZIONE IN A. P. · TASSA PAGATA · TARIFFA FATTURE
AUTORIZZAZIONE DCCP · 1 / 486 / ST DEL 12 · 3 · 1969

PER APRIRE SOLLEVARE E TIRARE IL LEMBO

A

La bolletta in dettaglio ③

UBICAZIONE IMPIANTO ④				
PREF.	N. TELEFONO	BOLLETTA	SCADENZA PAGAMENTO	IMPORTO
⑤	⑥	⑦		

⑩

VEDERE SUL RETRO DELLA FATTURA IL DETTAGLIO FISCALE DEI CODICI E DELLE ALIQUOTE IVA
L'imposta sul valore aggiunto, se presente ...
Fin. TC ... indicata ... non è ... presente perché relativo ...
riscuoter ...

SCATTI EFFETTUATI DAL 1 AGO
LETTURA AL ⑫
LETTURA AL ⑬
TOTALE SCATTI EFFETTUATI ⑭

COSTO DEGLI SCATTI ⑮
N.   SCATTI
N.   SCATTI
N.   SCATTI COMPLESSIVI

ATTENZIONE: STACCARE LUNGO IL TRATTEGGIO E CONSER

1. Issuing Office
2. Customer information
3. Breakdown of the bill
4. Location of apparatus
5. Telephone code
6. Telephone number
7. Bill number (e.g. 6th bimonthly bill of '92).
8. Pay-by-date
9. Amount
10. Notice as to whether payments are regular or not
11. Period during which points have been assessed
12. First reading
13. Last reading

Fig. 36. Telephone Bill

SI RICORDA CHE GLI UTENTI POSSONO RITIRARE LE BOLLETTE SENZA SPESE DI SPEDIZIONE PRESSO GLI UFFICI DELL'AGENZIA SIP TERRITORIALMENTE COMPETENTE, A PARTIRE DAL 1' GIORNO DI OGNI BIMESTRE DI FATTURAZIONE. IN TAL CASO, PER RAGIONI TECNICHE, GLI UTENTI INTERESSATI SONO PREGATI DI DARE TEMPESTIVA COMUNICAZIONE SCRITTA AI PREDETTI UFFICI, VALIDA FINO A REVOCA.

LA BOLLETTA PUÒ ESSERE PAGATA PRESSO LE CASSE ABILITATE DELLA SIP. GLI UFFICI POSTALI O - CON LE COMMISSIONI D'USO - PRESSO GLI SPORTELLI DI QUALSIASI BANCA. E ANCHE POSSIBILE INCARICARE LA PROPRIA BANCA DI PROVVEDERE AL PAGAMENTO DELLE BOLLETTE IN VIA CONTINUATIVA MEDIANTE ADDEBITO SUL CONTO.

PER INFORMAZIONI RIVOLGERSI: - AL 187 (LA TELEFONATA È GRATUITA)
- ALL'UFFICIO DELLA VOSTRA ZONA (GLI INDIRIZZI SONO INDICATI NELL'AVANTIELENCO)

) AL 1 OTTOBRE ⑪

_____

L.
L.

PER UN TOTALE DI L. ⑱

DETTAGLIO IMPORTI ⑭   LIRE   COD.

COSTO SCATTI DAL 1 AGOSTO   AL 1 OTTOBRE
IMPIANTO BASE:CANONE BIM.   NOVEMBRE-DICEMBRE
ACCESSORI:CANONE BIMESTRALE NOVEMBRE-DICEMBRE

SPEDIZIONE BOLLETTA
IVA
ARROTONDAMENTO BOLLETTA PRECEDENTE
ARROTONDAMENTO BOLLETTA ATTUALE   _____

                TOTALE BOLLETTA

⑳ ㉑ ㉒ ㉓ ㉔ ㉕ ㉖ ㉗

ARE LA FATTURA STAMPATA NEL MODULO DI VERSAMENTO.

---

14. Total points consumed
15. Cost of points at 50 Lit. each
17. Number of points at 127 Lit. each
18. Total cost of points
19. breakdown of costs
20. Cost of points in given period
21. Bi-monthly rent of apparatus
22. Bi-monthly rent of accessories

23. Delivery of bill
24. VAT
25. Rounding up of preceding bill
26. Rounding up of actual bill
27. Total bill

Heating options

The way you heat your home will depend largely whether you live in an urban or rural area. Urban properties, as mentioned above, usually have access to town gas and this is probably the most economic way to run central heating. If you do not have access to town gas economic alternatives include installing a *serbatoi* (gas tank) which will be filled directly from a lorry when necessary. There are usually several competing gas companies in an area, so you should shop around for estimates and also services before settling on any one. Many companies offer to give an estimate and asses where best to install the tank free of charge.

Regulations concerning the positioning of a gas tank stipulate that it must be at least 7 m from any houses and 15 m from public buildings. Competitive gas companies offer the actual tank free of charge (although it remains the company's property) and only bill the client for the gas that is delivered. To find gas companies look out for billboards along the roadsides in your locality or consult the *Pagine Gialle* (Yellow Pages), looking under Gas Compressi e Liquefatti.

If your property will not accommodate a gas tank and you live in or near a mountainous or forested area, you may consider using wood as your fuel. Italian rural homes often have a radiator inserted at the back of their fireplace which heats other radiators in the house and may even provide hot water. It is a good system but one that depends on keeping a fire alight.

Oil and electricity are both too highly priced to consider as economic forms of regular heating. Other alternatives include running gas fires from *bombola* (bottle gas). Bottle gas comes in cylinders of varying sizes, although the most common is the 40 kg. The same gas companies that supply gas tanks often sell gas bottles too. Terms of delivery and deposits paid on bottles may vary from company to company but the gas itself is sold at a fixed price, which is not particularly cheap and so is not a very good solution to regular heating.

6
Day-to-Day Living

SHOPS AND FACILITIES

Everyday life in Italy runs a very different course to that in the UK, partly
because of the opening times and partly because shops and other facilities
are simply not run in the same way. The British queue system breaks down
in the face of the Italian shop assistant who tries to serve a little to
everybody at one time. Instead of the UK's anonymous supermarket cash
desk, in Italy the shop is a place to catch up with the latest gossip and to
exchange civilities.

In Italy shopping and daily chores are a pleasure, provided you go
about them in an Italian way. This section enables you to do this and
supplies simple information that Italians take for granted, but that may be
alien to you.

Shops
General opening hours of shops are as follows:

8.30–9 am to 12.30– 1 pm, 4.30–5 pm to 7.30–8 pm

These hours apply Monday to Saturday inclusive. Sunday is closing day
for everyone except for shops selling fresh pasta and shops selling
newspapers, which open on Sunday morning. All shops have an early
closing day which varies depending on the type of shop it is and also the
region of Italy. Generally speaking, shops are closed on the following days
(except for those in tourist resorts where they often stay open seven days
a week and on public holidays too):

Monday—hairdressers, photographers, clothes boutiques and pasta shops
Tuesday or Wednesday or Thursday — food shops
Tuesday and Thursday afternoons — butchers (including those within
supermarkets)
Saturday — hardware/appliances shops

In the summer everybody takes a three-week holiday some time between June and October, the most popular month being August. When a shop is closed for a holiday you will find *chiuso per ferie* written on the doors usually with the date on which it will re-open.

Although supermarkets exist they are often quite small and have a limited selection, and shopping is mostly done in a series of individual shops. Most supermarkets are franchises of Sidis, Cral, Conad and the like, but they are still more like grocery stores than Italian versions of Sainsbury's or Tescos. Consequently high-street butchers, bakers and grocers are kept in business, as are other shops selling food, such as the fresh pasta shop and the café which usually produces an irresistible selection of cakes, patisserie and icecream as well as serving coffee and alcoholic drinks.

One of the most indispensable shops along the highstreet is the *tabacchi* (tobacconists). They sell the various necessities for dealing with bureaucracy, such as postage stamps, together with matches (which you will probably not find in either the supermarket or anywhere else), sweets, cigarettes, postcards, toiletries and a selection of gifts and souvenirs.

Something missing from the Italian high street is the laundrette. Nearly all Italian families have washing machines at home so there is no demand except in the biggest cities and where there is a high student or tourist population, such as in Florence. Dry cleaners may offer a washing service, but you will pay well above the odds for it. If you get really desperate, search out a wash-house in a village and do it yourself.

The following is a list of shops in Italian:

alimentari	food shop/grocer's
calzolaio	shoe repairer
casa di pasta	fresh pasta shop
enoteca	wine merchant's
farmacia	chemist's
ferramenta	hardware store
gelateria	icecream shop
gioielleria	jeweller's
macelleria	butcher's
mercato	market
paneficio/panetteria	baker's
parrucchiere	hairdresser
pasticceria	cake shop
pescheria	fish shop
profumeria	perfume shop

salumeria	salami and cured meats
supermercato	supermarket
tabacchi	tobacconist's
tintoria	dry cleaner's
ufficio postale	post office

Whatever you purchase while you are out shopping, whether it is a postcard or a pair of shoes, you will be given a *ricevuta fiscale* (receipt), which you should keep until reaching home in case the *guardia di finanza* (a branch of the police) should ask you to prove you purchased your goods and the shopkeeper registered the sale. This also applies to having a haircut or drinking a *cappuccino*, even though it would seem almost impossible to prove the expenditure. Should you not be given a receipt, officially both you and the seller are liable to a fine.

Banks

Italian banks are open Monday to Friday only, 8.30 am–1.30 pm. Some also open in the afternoon, usually between 3 and 4 pm, although this varies slightly from bank to bank. The majority of banks operate on a local rather than a national basis, which means that services are not very wide-ranging. For example, you are unlikely to be able to use your Italian cheque book outside your region, or possibly even your local town. (See Fig. 37, showing how to fill in an Italian cheque; write *non-trasferibile* across the back if you want it to be non-transferable.) Note that it is very common not to write either the date or to whom the cheque is payable.

Apart from the convenience of having bills directly debited and making transfers of money from overseas, an Italian bank account has little to recommend it, accruing as it does a host of expenses and tax charges, including an annual tax of 20 per cent. Many Italians have safes at home, usually in the wall behind a painting, and keep their money that way. Fortunately, the pressure of the EC free market has obliged banks to develop computer link-ups and install automatic cash machines which take international cards, opening up access to foreign banks.

To open an Italian bank account you will probably have to have an interview with the bank manager, or his secretary, and produce the following documents:

- *certificato di residenza*;
- *codice fiscale*;
- passport or identity card.

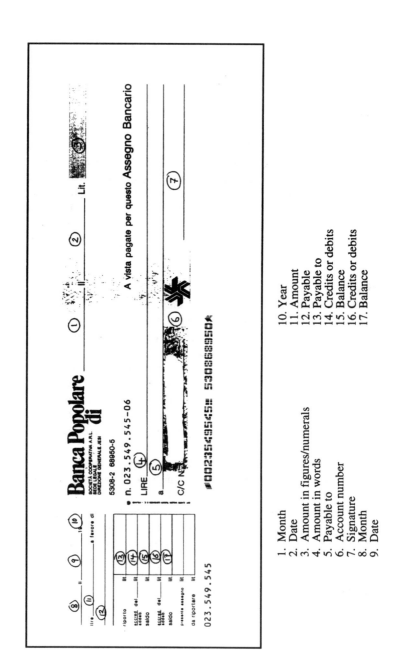

1. Month
2. Date
3. Amount in figures/numerals
4. Amount in words
5. Payable to
6. Signature
7. Month
8. Month
9. Date
10. Year
11. Amount
12. Payable
13. Payable to
14. Credits or debits
15. Balance
16. Credits or debits
17. Balance

Fig. 37. Facsimile of cheque.

Check out the facilities available at the bank during your interview. Some of the basic facilities include:

- *cartasi* or other credit card;
- *bancomat* cash card;
- cheque book.

Also check on the bank charges, interest rates and annual taxes that are levied. If you are a non-resident you will be liable to higher charges and taxes, and will not have all the facilities that are available to residents, such as having bills directly debited.

Once you have opened an account, all charges and transactions are written on a very complicated monthly statement. The facsimile shown in Fig. 38 may help you to decipher it.

Post offices

The post office, known as the PTT or *ufficio postale*, as well as providing regular postal services is the place where most people pay bills, transfer postal orders, collect their pensions, pay for their car tax and so on. Not surprisingly, therefore, there are invariably long queues and if you simply want to buy a postage stamp you are much better off going to a *tabacchi*.

As the post office is open government hours, generally 8 am–2 pm (although major post offices are open 12 hours a day), the lunch period is the quietest time to go. To send a parcel you may have to go to a special parcel post office where you must fill in a form, usually at least in triplicate, giving details of both the sender *(mittente)* and the receiver *(destinario)*.

Most post offices are fussy about the way in which you package a parcel; the preferred method is to use string and a metal seal which can be purchased from a *cartolibreria* (book shop) or *tabacchi* (tobacconist).

You may wish to use the post office to receive mail by *poste restante*. The sender should address the envelope *fermo posta* followed by the address of the post office. You will probably need to show an identity document to claim post and may have to pay a charge. The post office also send telegrams and deals with money orders.

Information regarding postal services is obtainable by dialing 160.

GETTING AROUND

Italy has a fairly well-used and well-priced but poorly organised public-transport system. Strikes, delays and technical hitches regularly wreak

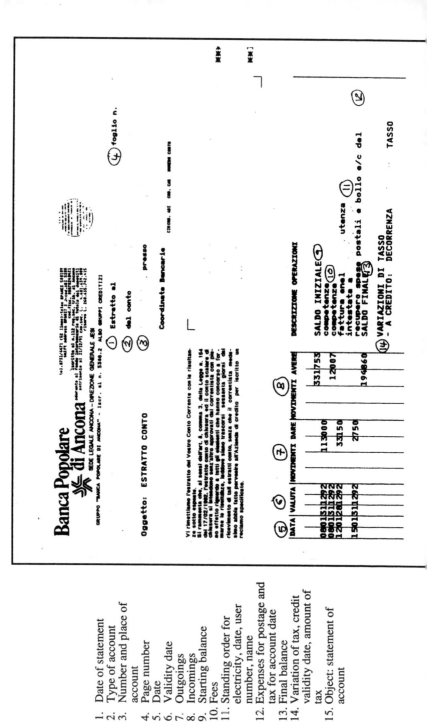

Fig. 38. Bank statement

1. Date of statement
2. Type of account
3. Number and place of account
4. Page number
5. Date
6. Validity date
7. Outgoings
8. Incomings
9. Starting balance
10. Fees
11. Standing order for electricity, date, user number, name
12. Expenses for postage and tax for account date
13. Final balance
14. Variation of tax, credit validity date, amount of tax
15. Object: statement of account

Cod. LB55N

Desideriamo rammentare alle Gentile Clientela che il Conto
Corrente e', tra l'altro, un validissimo strumento per pagare,
risparmiando sui costi, tasse e utenze di vario genere (Enel,
Sip, Metano, Acqua, etc.), alle scadenze previste...
senz'affanno ne' code.

Banca Popolare di Ancona

Banca Popolare di Ancona
IL DIRETTORE GENERALE

chaos. Private transport companies are better run, but it tends to be the case that all buses and trains for the same destination leave at the same time, rendering the selection of services somewhat limited. It is hardly surprising, therefore, that most Italians travel by car. This section gives information both on the public-transport system and on running a car in Italy.

Railway

The state railway, *Ferrovie Statale*, is probably public transport at its worst. Despite a fairly wide network, covering some 16,000 km, services generally leave much to be desired. Most trains are slow by European standards, the ticket system is abominably complicated and inefficient, and strikes often grind the whole system to a halt. Fares are calculated according to class, distance travelled, and the type of train. The main types are listed as follows, in order of cost and speed:

- ETR 450 Pendolino;
- Intercity;
- Express;
- Diretto;
- Locale.

If you buy your ticket on the train you will have to pay a surcharge of 20 per cent. If you purchase a ticket but do not use it, it is possible to obtain a refund, providing you return it to the station from which you bought it on the day for which your ticket is valid. For trains that are delayed for more than 29 minutes, refunds are also offered of any supplements or surcharges that have been paid. The refund will be given in the form of a coupon that can be used on subsequent rail travel.

Telephone numbers of the principal railway information offices are as follows:

Bologna	(051) 372126
Bolzano	(0471) 24292
Cagliari	(070) 656293
Catania	(095) 531625
Florence	(055) 278785
Genoa	(010) 284081

Livorno	(0586) 401105
Messina	(090) 775234
Milan	(02) 67500
Naples	(081) 5534188
Padua	(049) 6161806
Palermo	(091) 230806
Pisa	(050) 41385
Prato	(0574) 26617
Reggio Calabria	(0965) 98123
Rimini	(0541) 53512
Rome	(06) 4775
Savona	(019) 806969
Turin	(011) 517551

Coach and bus

All rural districts are serviced by local bus networks. Tickets are available either from the bus station or on the bus itself. Cities also have private bus networks and some have trams too. Here tickets, which are at a fixed rate regardless of distance covered, are sold at bus stations, *tabacchi* (tobacconists) and at newspaper kiosks where you can see the sign *biglietti*. Rome, Milan and Naples have a *metropolitana* (underground train) too. Tickets for the *metropolitana* are sold at train stations and like buses have a flat rate fare.

Express coach services provide a good alternative to travelling by train for any long distance. Fares are relatively inexpensive and services are fairly frequent. Information on timetables is held at local tourist offices and sometimes at local police stations, as well as being posted up at the bus depot itself.

Ferries

If you have a property on the coast or on one of the northern lakes you will undoubtedly make use of the local ferries and hydrofoils which are an efficient and usually enjoyable way to get around. The main sea crossings are from the mainland to Sardinia and Sicily, details of which can be obtained from the UK addresses as follows:

Tirrenia Line and Navarma
c/o Serena Holidays
40–42 Kenway Road
London SW5 0RA
Tel: (071) 373 6548.

Grandi Traghetti
Associated Oceanic Agencies
103–105 Jermyn Street
London SW1Y 6EE
Tel: (071) 930 5683.

There are umpteen other services to other offshore islands including
the Aeolian islands, Capri, Elba and Giglio. The northern lakes are also
traversed by innumerable services, including hydrofoils, car-ferries and
even steamers, as many people commute from one side of the lake to the
other or travel to school that way.

Air

Alitalia is Italy's principal airway. Its sister company, ATI, operates
domestic services between 26 cities in Italy with regular flights from
Alghero, Bologna, Cagliari, Genoa, Naples, Olbia, Palermo, Pisa and
Venice to Rome and Milan. The head offices for Alitalia and Ati are as
follows, although flight bookings are taken at any authorised travel agents:

Alitalia
Palazzo Alitalia
Piazzale G. Pastore
EUR
Rome
Information, Tel: (06) 5456
Domestic flight reservations, Tel: (06) 5455.

Ati
Palazzo Ati
Aeroporto Capodichino
Naples
Information and reservations, Tel: (081) 7091111.

Buying a car

Buying a car in Italy, particularly second-hand, is considerably more
expensive than buying one in the UK. However, the problems and expense
involved in having a non-local car, which means from outside your
provincial region let alone from overseas, are not worth entertaining. Go
to the salesrooms in your locality, some of which will sell *usate* (second-
hand cars) as well as *nuove* (new) and look through the classified adverts
in the local papers.

Points to take into consideration when choosing a car, other than technical ones, include the previous owner's road tax situation, and the cost of the year's road tax, which for diesel, four-wheeled-drive vehicles, campers and high-powered bikes is considerable, ranging from about £300 to £900. If road tax payments are not up to date then you will find that you are liable for back payments when you go to renew it.

The buying procedure is quite straightforward provided you have the two following documents:

- *certificato di residenza*
- *codice fiscale*

If you are buying a car privately both you and the seller, along with the above documents, will need to go to an ACI office where the necessary papers will be drawn up for the transfer of ownership. Otherwise these formalities are carried out in car salesrooms.

Non-residents can only purchase a vehicle direct from the manufacturer and are obliged to export it within a year of purchase.

Should you decide to buy a car that does not have a local number plate, that is without the *sigla* (initials) of the province in which you are resident, you will have to have it re-registered, a procedure that costs in the region of 900,000Lit. at the time of writing. Registration plates are the work of the *Motorizazzione Civile*, although your local Automobile Club Italiano (ACI) will deal with the matter.

Running a car

Other than fuel, repair and maintenance, the two main costs in running a car in Italy are insurance and road tax, the documents for both of which must be displayed in your windscreen.

Insurance, which is obligatory at least for third party is often sold by ACI (Automobile Club Italiano) as well as insurance agents. It is worth shopping around for a policy, as once you have signed you are obliged to keep with that company for ten years unless you give six months' notice. The most common form of insurance operates on a no-claims bonus known as **bonus malus**. Note that third-party insurance generally does not cover the driver, only family members in the car. Cover for the driver, **Conducente anonimo**, can be taken out in the form of a supplement. Additional premiums are also required for theft and fire.

Road tax must be paid at the post office on an official *bollo* (chit). If your car has been in circulation for any time you will have a large cheque book of these *bollo*, otherwise they are obtainable from ACI. Each *bollo*

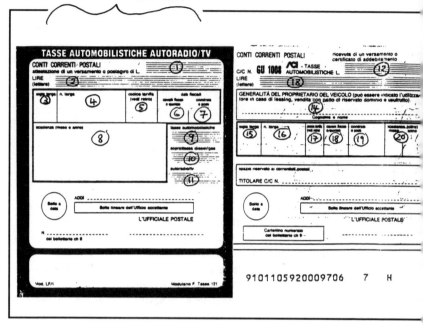

1. Total amount of tax paid in numerals
2. Total amount of tax paid in letters
3. Initials of province on number plate
4. Number plate
5. Tariff code
6. Horse power
7. Number of cylinders
8. Expiry date
9. Car tax
10. Extra tax for diesel or gas
11. Tax for car radio or TV
12. As 1
13. As 2
14. Surname and name of car owner
15. As 3
16. As 4
17. As 5
18. As 6
19. As 7
20. Expiry date (month and year)
21. Total amount of tax paid in numerals

Fig. 39. Car tax 'bollo'

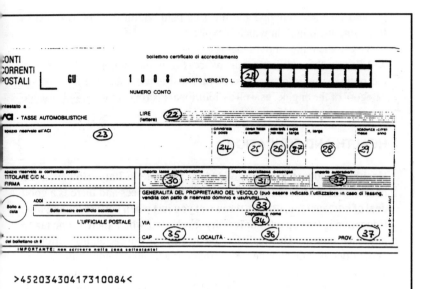

>45203430417310084<

22. Total amount of tax paid in letters
23. Space reserved for ACI (Automobile Club Italiano)
24. As 7
25. As 6
26. As 5
27. As 3
28. As 4
29. As 20
30. As 9
31. As 10
32. As 11
33. As 14
34. Address - Street
35. Post code
36. Place
37. Province

is valid for three months, and must be paid within the first two weeks following the month in which it expires.

To calculate the amount that is due you should consult the charts you will find on the wall in the post office. Fill in the appropriate figures on the *bollo*, namely for the type of fuel that is used, and the horsepower category of the engine, as well as additional tax for car radios and cassette players, as in the example shown in Fig. 39.

HEALTH AND EDUCATION

Health and education are provided by the state in Italy. However, the health system offers little in the way of free services and there is a good deal of bureaucracy, usually thrown at you just when you are feeling low. Education is free up until university level, after which there is one tax to pay after another. The quality of the health and education institutions is generally lower than in the UK, perhaps as a result of undue bureaucracy and underfunding; however, there are always notable exceptions. If you are planning on staying in Italy for any period of time you will probably find sending your children to an Italian school and using the health services perfectly adequate, although it depends rather upon where you live, the south of Italy having a lower standard of living than the north.

Health system

Health care in Italy is offered in return for an annual contribution, tassa disaluta, which is assessed according to your salary. If you are still resident in the UK then you should obtain form E111 before leaving from your unemployment benefit office which entitles you to state health care. If you are a new resident in Italy you will have to wait for your first tax return before your contributions are adjusted to your salary. Otherwise you will pay the fixed voluntary contribution for foreigners of 750,000Lit. per family unit.

Once you are settled into your new home you should locate your local USL (Unita Locale Sanitaria) which deals with state Health care and go along to register. In order to do this take along the following documents:

- identity document;
- *stato di famiglia*;
- *certificato di residenza*;
- *codice fiscale* (fiscal code card;)
- letter from employer declaring employment;

or
- *attesta di iscrizione* (inscription card from unemployment office);
- *permesso di soggiorno* (permit to stay).

At the same time as registering you will be asked to select a family doctor from the official list as well as a paediatrician if you have children under the age of six. Once the registration is completed you will be issued with a **tessera sanitaria** (health card), a document that entitles you to public health care. The *tessera* has to be renewed annually, which means taking along all the documents in the above list again. Should you lose your *tessera* apply to USL immediately for a duplicate.

Education
Schooling is free from the age of 3 to 19 to all residents, provided they can speak Italian. Education is only compulsory from the age of 6 up until the age of 14, after which children generally go to a vocational school or continue with a classical education that generally leads up to university. There is a national curriculum laid down by the Ministero della Pubblica Istruzione (Ministry of Public Education), but management and administration are locally organised.

The school year runs from mid-September to mid-June with short holidays at Christmas and Easter and no half-term breaks. Most classes are in the mornings, but there is school six days a week. From primary level upwards, students are expected to spend their afternoons doing homework and private study.

Low-achieving children and those with minor handicaps are integrated in normal classes, but usually have a special teacher who dedicates extra time within the class.

The following are the various schools that exist within the state system and the ages of the pupils they cater for:

- *scuola materna* (nursery school) 3–6;
- *scuola elementare* (elementary school) 6–10;
- *scuola media* (middle school) 11–14;
- *scuola secondaria di II grado* (upper secondary school) 15–19.

There are five basic types of upper secondary school:

- *liceo classico* (classics lyceum);
- *liceo scientifico* (scientific lyceum);
- *liceo artistico* (artistic lyceum);

- *istituto tecnico* (technical institute);
- *istituto professionale* (vocational institute).

The classics and scientific schools tend to be attended by students who intend to go on to university. The technical and vocational institutes tend to lead directly to specific careers. However, all graduates of any secondary education are eligible for university entry.

Appendix of Further Information

USEFUL ADDRESSES ABROAD AND UK

Italian cultural institutes

Italian Cultural Institute
39 Belgrave Square
London SW1X 8NT
UK
Tel: (071) 235 1461.

Italian Cultural Institute
82 Nicholson Street
Edinburgh EH3 7HW
UK.

British Italian Society
172 Regent Street
5th Floor
London W1
UK.

British Italian Society
24 Rutland Gate
London SW7 1BB
UK
Tel: (071) 823 9204.

Italian Cultural Institute
Fitzwilliam Square 11
Dublin
Eire.

Italian Cultural Institute
1601 Fuller Street NW
Washington DC 20009
USA.

Italian Cultural Institute
686 Park Avenue
New York NY 10021
USA.

Italian Cultural Institute
500 North Michigan Avenue
Suite 530
Chicago IL 60611
USA.

Italian Cultural Institute
225 Bush Street No 310
San Francisco
CA 94108
USA.

Italian Cultural Institute
12400 Wilshire Boulevard
Suite 310
Los Angeles
CA 90025
USA.

Italian Cultural Institute
275 Slater Street
Ottawa KIP 5IP
Canada.

Italian Cultural Institute
1200 Penfield Drive
Montreal
Quebec H3A 1A9
Canada.

Italian Cultural Institute
496 Huron Street
Toronto
Canada.

Italian Cultural Institute
208-1200 Burrard Street
Vancouver B6Z 2CT
Canada.

Italian consulates and embassies

Italian Consulate General
38 Eaton Place
London SW1X 8AN.
UK
Tel: (071) 235 9371.

Italian Embassy
14 Three Kings Yard
London W1
UK
Tel: (071) 629 8200.

Italian Consulate
6 Melville Crescent
Edinburgh
UK.

Italian Consulate
111 Piccadilly
Manchester
UK.

Italian Vice-Consulate
23 Allhallows
Bedford
UK.

Italian Embassy
63 Northumberland Road
Dublin
Eire.

Italian Embassy
275 Slater Street
11th Floor
Ottawa KIP 5H9
Canada.

Italian Embassy
1601 Fuller Street NW
Washington DC 20009
USA.

Italian state tourism offices

Italian State Tourist Office
1 Princes Street
London W1R 8AY
UK
Tel: (071) 408 1254.

Italian State Tourist Office
47 Merrion Square
Dublin
Eire.

Italian State Tourism Office
3M9
1 Place Ville Marie
Suite 1914
Montreal
Quebec HEB
Canada.

Italian State Tourist Office
  630 Fifth Avenue
  Suite 1565
  New York
  NY10111
  USA.

Italian trade institutes

Italian Trade Centre (ICE)
  37 Sackville Street
  London W1X 2DQ
  UK
  Tel: (071) 734 2412.

Italian Chamber of Commerce
  Room 418-427 Walmar House
  296 Regent Street
  London W1R 5HB
  UK
  Tel: (071) 637 3153.

Italian Institute for Foreign Trade
  16 St Stephen's Green
  Dublin
  Eire.

Other useful addresses

The Royal Scottish Automobile
  Club
  11 Blythwood Square
  Glasgow G2 4AG
  UK.

Royal Automobile Club
  PO Box 100
  RAC House
  Landsdowne Road
  Croydon CR9 2JA
  UK.

Automobile Association
  Fanum House
  PO Box 51
  Basingstoke
  Hants RG21 2BH
  Tel: (0256) 469777.

Department of Social Security
  Overseas Branch
  Newcastle Upon Tyne
  NE98 1YX
  UK.

Animal Health Division 1B
  Government Buildings
  Hook Rise South
  Kingston By-Pass
  Surbiton
  Surrey KT6 7NF
  UK.

USEFUL ADDRESSES IN ITALY

Foreign consulates and embassies

British Embassy
  Via XX Settembre 80/A
  Rome
  Tel: (06) 4755441.

British Consulate
  Accademia
  Dorsoduro 1051
  Venice
  Tel: (041) 5227207/5227408.

British Consulate
  Via San Lucifero 87
  Cagliari
  Tel: (070) 662750.

British Consulate
  Palazzo Castelbarco
  Lungarno Corsini 2
  Florence
  Tel: (055) 284133.

British Consulate
  Via XII Ottobre 2
  Genoa
  Tel: (010) 564833.

British Consulate
  Via San Paolo 7
  Milan
  Tel: (02) 803442.

British Consulate
  Via Francesco Crispi 122
  Naples
  Tel: (081) 663511.

British Consulate
  Via delle Ville 15
  Trieste
  Tel: (040) 302884.

Canadian Embassy
  Via G. B. de Rossi 27
  Rome
  Tel: (06) 445981.

Irish Embassy
  Largo del Nazareno 3
  Rome
  Tel: (06) 6782541.

USA Embassy
  Via Vittorio Veneto 119/A
  Rome
  Tel: (06) 46741.

British Council
  Via IV Fontane 20
  Rome.

Ministries

Ministero della Pubblica Istruzione
  (Ministry of Public Education)
  Viale Trastevere 76
  Rome.

Ministero degli Affari Esteri
  (Ministry of Foreign Affairs)
  Ufficio IX
  Piazzale della Farnesina
  Rome.

Youth information centres

Informagiovani
  Via Galimberti 2/a
  Alessandria
  Tel: (0131) 223366.

Informagiovani
  Via Paleocapa 2
  Bergamo
  Tel: (035) 238187.

Centro Informazione e
  Orientamento Professionale
  Via Zamboni 8
  Bologna
  Tel: (051) 218328.

Centro Informazione Giovani
  Piazza Vittoria 5
  Brescia
  Tel: (030) 2983505.

Centro Informagiovani
Piazza Dante 4
Caserta
Tel: (0832) 322822.

Servizio Informagiovani
Vicolo Santa Maria Maggiore 1
Florence
Tel: (055) 218310.

Centro Incontro
Via Pisana 578
Florence
Tel: (055) 713320.

Informagiovani
Via Goldoni 83
Livorno
Tel: (586) 50586.

Osmeg-Informshop
Via Vivaio 1
Milan
Tel: (02) 77402827.

Lombardia Lavoro
Via Ponchielli 24
Milan
Tel: (02) 29404675.

Centro Informazione Giovani
Via Scudari 8
Modena
Tel: (059) 206705.

Centro Informazioni
Documentazione Giovani
Corso Cavallotti 20
Novara
Tel: (0321) 23146.

Informagiovani
Vicolo Ponte Molino 7
Padua
Tel: (049) 654328.

Informagiovani
Via Oberdan 57
Pisa
Tel: (050) 595315.

Centro Informagiovani
Via del Can Bianco
Pistoia
Tel: (0573) 32928.

Centro Informagiovani
Via Mazzini 8
Ravenna.

Progetto Giovani
Via Mentana 9
Rimini
Tel: (0541) 24142.

National Secretariat
Coordinamento Nazionale
Sistema Informativo Giovanile
Via Palermo 28
Rome
Tel: (06) 4818089.

Informagiovani
Via G. Castano 29/31
Rome
Tel: (06) 2002635.

Informagiovani
Via Assarotti 2
Turin
Tel: (011) 57653572.

Servizio Orientamento
  Informagiovani
  Piazza Giovane Italia 6
  Varese
  Tel: (0322) 241565.

Centro Informagiovani
  Corso Portoni Borsari 17
  Verona
  Tel: (045) 597815.

Informagiovani Comune de
  Vicenza
  Contra San Tommaso 7
  Vicenza
  Tel: (0444) 228875.

Other useful addresses

Automobile Club Italiano
  Via Marsala 8
  Rome
  Tel: (06) 4212.

ABBREVIATIONS OF PROVINCES

The following is an alphabetical list of the abbreviations that are used for each of Italy's 95 provinces. You will see the abbreviations appear as the first two letters on car registration plates, in post codes and in official documents.

AG	Agrigento
AL	Alessandria
AN	Ancona
AO	Aosta
AP	Ascoli Piceno
AQ	Aquila
AR	Arezzo
AT	Asti
AV	Avellino
BA	Bari
BG	Bergamo
BL	Belluno
BN	Benevento
BO	Bologna
BR	Brindisi
BS	Brescia
BZ	Bolzano
CA	Cagliari
CB	Campobasso
CE	Caserta
CH	Chieti
CL	Caltanisetta
CN	Cuneo
CO	Como
CR	Cremona
CS	Cosenza
CT	Catania
CZ	Catanzaro
EN	Enna
FE	Ferrara
FG	Foggia
FI	Firenze
FO	Forli
FR	Frosinone
GE	Genova
GO	Gorizia
GR	Grosseto
IM	Imperia
IS	Isernia
LE	Lecce
LI	Livorno
LT	Latina
LU	Lucca
MC	Macerata
ME	Messina
MI	Milano

MN	Mantova	TV	Treviso
MO	Modena	UD	Udine
MS	Massa Carrara	VA	Varese
MT	Matera	VC	Vercelli
NA	Napoli	VE	Venezia
NO	Novara	VI	Vicenza
NU	Nuoro	VR	Verona
OR	Oristano	VT	Viterbo
PA	Palermo		
PC	Piacenza		
PD	Padova		

ALPHABET BY NAMES

The following alphabetical list is used by all Italians to spell out words, especially over the telephone.

PE	Pescara	A	Ancona
PG	Perugia	B	Bologna
PI	Pisa	C	Como
PN	Pordenone	D	Domodossola
PR	Parma	E	Empoli
PS	Pesaro	F	Firenze
PT	Pistoia	G	Genoa
PV	Pavia	H	Hotel
PZ	Potenza	I	Imola
RA	Ravenna	K	Kursaal
RC	Reggio Calabria	L	Livorno
RE	Reggio Emilia	M	Milano
RG	Ragusa	N	Napoli
RI	Rieti	O	Otranto
RO	Rovigo	P	Padova
ROMA	Roma	Q	Quarto
SA	Salerno	R	Roma
SI	Siena	S	Savona
SO	Sondrio	T	Torino
SP	Spezia	U	Udine
SR	Siracusa	V	Venezia
SS	Sassari	W	Washington
SV	Savona	X	Ics
TA	Taranto	Y	York or Yacht
TE	Teramo	Z	Zara
TN	Trento		
TO	Torino		
TP	Trapani		
TR	Terni		
TS	Trieste		

Glossary

PARTS OF A HOUSE

The following vocabulary list is made up of the various parts of a property.

angolo cottura	cooking corner
autorimessa	garage
bagno	bathroom
balcone	balcony
camera	room
camera doppio	bedroom with twin beds
camera matrimoniale	bedroom with double bed
camera singolo	bedroom with single bed
cameretta	small bedroom
camino	fireplace
cantina	cellar
corridoio	hall
cortile	courtyard
cucina	kitchen
cucina abitabile	kitchen/living-room
cucinotto	small kitchen
doccia	shower
doppi servizi	two bathrooms
doppio garage	double garage
garage	garage
giardino	garden
ingresso	entrance hall
interrato	basement
lavanderia	laundry
mansarda	attic
piscina	swimming pool
portico	porch

posto auto/macchina	parking space
ripostiglio	junk room
sala	room
salone	sitting-room
salotto	living-room
scala	staircase
soffitta	loft
soggiorno	sitting-room
soggiorno pranzo	living/dining-room
stanza	room
studio	study
terratetto	ground to roof
terrazza	terrace
tinello	small dining-room
ultimo piano	last floor
vani	room

TYPES OF HOUSING

The following vocabulary list is made up of the various terms used to describe the different types of housing.

allogio	accommodation
appartamento	flat
appartamento su due piani	flat on two floors
appartamento vacanze	holiday flat
azienda agricola	farm
bifamiliare	semi-detached
bilocale	2 rooms
3-locale	3 rooms
4-locale	4 rooms
5-locale	5 rooms
capannone	barn
casa	house
casa colonica	farmhouse
casa padronale	country house
casale	hamlet
casetta	small house
fabricato	building
fabricato rurale	rural building
fattoria	farm

indipendente	detached
monolocale	detached
palazzo	large building
rustico	rustic building
villa	detached house
villina	small detached house

PASSPORTS, VISAS AND PERMITS

certificato di equipollenza	certificate of academic equivalence
certificato di residenza	residence permit
cittadino	nationality
codice fiscale	fiscal code number
domicilio	address
firma	signature
giorno	day
nome, cognome	forename, surname
passaporto	passport
permesso di soggiorno	permit to stay
scopo lavorativo	for the purpose of work
scopo residenza	for the purpose of residence
sottoscritto	undersigned
Ufficio Anagrafe	Municipal Registry Office
Ufficio Collocamento	Italian Employment Office
Ufficio Imposte Dirette	Provincial Tax Office
Ufficio Stranieri	Foreign Department
valido (fino al)	valid (until)

TRAVEL

abbonamento	season ticket
Automobile Club d'Italia (ACI)	Italian Automobile Club
autostrada	motorway
benzina normale/super	regular/super grade petrol
biglietto, biglietti, biglietteria	ticket, tickets/ticket office
Carta Verde	Youth Rail Card
chilometrico	ticket allowing 3,000km free rail travel
conducento anonimo	unnamed driver
corso	main street, boulevard
entrata	entrance

Ferrovie Statale	State Railway System
mezza pensione	half board
Ministero del Trasporto	Ministry of Transport
numero targa	number plate
incrocio	crossroads
lavori in corso	road works ahead
passaggio a livello	level crossing
pensione	boarding houses
pericolo	danger
rallentare	slow down
scheda tecnica	schedule of technical data on a vehicle
senso vietato	no entry
senso unico	one way
sosta autorizzato	parking permitted at certain times
sosta vietato	no parking
strada (privata)	road (private)
uscita	exit
verde	lead-free petrol
verde verde	higher octane lead-free petrol
viacard	motorway toll card
zona blu	parking within blue lines only
zona disco	parking within restricted times
zona rimozione	no parking: cars will be towed away
zona tutelato	no parking either side of road
vietato ingresso	no entry

MONEY MATTERS

bollo	chit or state stamp
bonus/malus	insurance policy based on no claims bonuses
buste	payslips
camera di commercio	chamber of commerce
commercialista	book-keeper, accountant
denuncia	statement; income tax return
franchigia	insurance policy with excess limit
gettone	token (eg for pay phones)
imposte	tax
ricevuta fiscale	receipt

Scala mobili	wage indexation
tangenti	kick-backs, bribes
ufficio imposte dirette	provincial tax office

GENERAL

agenzia	agent, agency
alimentari	grocery stores
antiquario	antique shop
calzolaio	shoe repairer
Carta Si	an Italian credit card
cartolibreria	bookshop
casa del formaggio	cheese shop
casa di pasta	pasta shop
comune, municipio	town hall
denuncia	legal/police statement
elenchi telefonici	telephone directories
enoteca	wine merchant
fai da te	DIY
farmacia	chemist
ferramenta	hardware store
francobolli	postage stamp
gabinetti	WC
gelateria	ice cream shop
macelleria	butcher's shop
mercato	market
paneficio/panetteria	bakery
parrucchiere	hairdresser
passeggiata	evening stroll or promenade
pescheria	fishmonger
profumeria	perfumery
saldi	sales
signore, signori	ladies, gentlemen
supermercato	supermarket
tabacchi	tobacconists
tintoria	drycleaner
toiletta	WC
tribunale	magistrates court
ufficio postale	post office
vigili urbani	town police

Further Reading

GENERAL

How to Get a Job in Europe, Mark Hempshell (How To Books 1992).
How to Live & Work in Italy, Amanda Hinton (How To Books, 1993).
How to Retire Abroad, Roger Jones (How To Books, 1993).
Working Abroad: Essential Financial Planning for Expatriates and their Employers, Jonathan Golding (International Venture Handbooks, Plymbridge Distributors, Plymouth).
Getting It Right in Italy: A Manual for the 1990s, William Ward (Bloomsbury, 1990).
Italy 1993 (Fodor Gold Guide Series, 1992).

PROPERTY

Setting Up in Italy, Sebastian O'Kelly (Merehurst Press, 1990).
Your Home in Italy, F. Maxwell (Longman Professional, 1989).
Urban Land and Property Markets in Italy, Gastone Ave (UCLP, 1993).
Doing Business in Italy, Dalbert Hallenstein (BBC Books, 1991).
Gardens of the Italian Villas, Marcella Agnelli (Weidenfeld & Nicolson, 1987).
Italy: Practical Commercial Law Roberto Barbalich (Longman, 1991).
Italian Living Design: Three Decades of Interiors, Giuseppi Raimondi (Taurus Parke, 1990). Translated from the Italian.
Italian Splendour: Palaces, Castles & Villas, Jack Basehart (Rizzoli, 1990).

REGIONAL GUIDES

Italian Journeys, Jonathan Keates (Picador, 1992).
A Place in Italy, Simon Mawer (Sinclair Stevenson, 1992).
Italy: Insight Guides Series (APA Publications, 1992).

Southern Italy: From Rome to Calabria, Paul Blanchard (Blue Guides, 1990).
Baedeker's Italy (Automobile Association, 1993).
Tuscany, Umbria and the Marches, Michael Pauls & Dana Facaros (Cadagon, 1992).
Southern Italy: A Traveller's Guide, Paul Holberton (Murray, 1992).
Lombardy: The Italian Lakes John Flower (Philip, 1990).
Milan, Richard Sale (Crowood, 1991).
Italy: Off the Beaten Track Series, Richard Sale (Moorland, 1993).
Italy by Train, Tim Jepson (Hodder & Stoughton, 1993).
Umbria: Maps and Plans, Alta Macadam (Blue Guides, 1993).
Rome: American Express Pocket Guides, Anthony Pereira & Nick Skidmore (Mitchell Beazley, 1992).
Florence and Tuscany, Sheila Hale (Mitchell Beazley, 1992).
Venice and the Veneto, James Bentley (Aurum, 1992).
Italy: The Hill Towns, James Bentley (George Philip, 1990).
Visitor's Guide to Northern Italy, Amanda Hinton (Moorland, 1992).
Visitor's Guide to Southern Italy, Amanda Hinton (Moorland, 1993).

Index

Other Books in this Series

How to Live & Work in America
Steve Mills BA(Hons) MA

America today is the number one destination for British and other expatriates. This highly readable and informative handbook explains America's rules and regulations on immigration: a jungle of quotas, green cards and special categories, plus work and lifestyle prospects in this ultimate land of opportunity. Steve Mills lectures at the University of Keele Centre for American Studies and has worked extensively in America. 'A mine of information.' *The Expatriate*.

244pp illustrated paperback. 1 85703 058 3. Second Edition.

How to Live & Work in Australia
Laura Veltman

The *Sydney-Sun-Herald* reported a massive 1,400 telephone calls a day to Australia House in London from would-be immigrants from Britain, with queues of personal callers stretching round the block. Never has there been such competition to get in. If *you* are competing of a place, *you* need **How to Live & Work in Australia**, packed from cover to cover with vital current information on costs, the crucial 'points' system, job opportunities, essential addresses, and domestic living in Australia today. 'One marvellous book. . . has just been published. . . it's written by Australian journalist Laura Veltman and she should know what she's talking about as she specialises in Australian migrant affairs. Written in a clear and entertaining style it provides all sorts of information (and) there's great good humour as Laura takes an honest look at Australian attitudes.' *Resident Abroad magazine*. 'Of interest to young travellers, too.' *The Times*. 'There has never been a better time to get hold of **How to Live & Work in Australia**.' *Southern X*.

240pp illustrated paperback. 1 85703 057 5. Third Edition.

How to Live & Work in Belgium
Marvina Shilling

Researched and written by a specialist on Belgian affairs, this is a complete manual of essential information on Belgium from entering the country to taking up residence, coping with the language, living in Brussels, Antwerp and other major cities, understanding the business, official and legal environment, the cost of living and other vital facts and advice for executives, officials, technicians, students, teachers and others. 'Interesting, easy to read and full of fascinating information . . . Gives a succinct and enlightening explanation for the use of both the French and Dutch language and the political tensions engendered by this language split.' *Phoenix/Association of Graduate Careers Advisory Services*. 'A crisp and clear resumé. . . If companion volumes are on a similar par, a European collection would be particularly appropriate.' *Newscheck/ Careers Service Bulletin*.

139pp illustrated. 1 85703 053 2.

How to Live & Work in France
Nicole Prevost Logan

This book meets the need for a clear compendium of information and advice for longer-stay visitors or residents, whether their interests are commercial, official, technical, educational or lifestyle/retirement. It includes an extensive contacts section covering embassies and consulates, travel contacts, business contacts (including banks) in both Britain and France, and miscellaneous key addresses. Nicole Prevost Logan became licensed in Law at the University of Paris and obtained the Diploma in Political Science from the Institut D'Etudes Politiques. An experienced teacher, cultural adviser and student counsellor, she presently teaches French language and civilisation. 'A welcome addition to the list.' *Franco-British Society Newsletter*.

160pp illustrated paperback. 1 85703 082 6. Second Edition.

How to Live & Work in Germany
Nessa Loewenthal

West and East Germany formally became a single nation in October 1990. The real work of unification is likely to take many years, but this process — added to the ultimate potential for economic and cultural growth — makes this an exciting time to live in Germany. Whether you are planning to relocate for three months of three years, this is the book for you. It covers such practical topics as entry requirements, transportation, money matters, housing, schools, insurance and much besides. It also includes valuable pointers to German values, customs, business practices and etiquette to help you make the most of your stay. Nessa Loewenthal is Director of Trans Cultural Services, and a consultant specialising in intercultural briefing. 'Detailed help is given on how to find work in Germany including . . . a comprehensive list of organisations which offer the chance to combine the experience of living in Germany with a useful activity.' *Phoenix/Association of Graduate Careers Advisory Services.*

142pp illustrated. 1 85703 006 0.

How to Live & Work in Hong Kong
Martin Bennett

Hong Kong is one of the most dynamic centres in the world, and despite the shadow now hanging over its future, it remains an important centre for expatriates. This book will be essential reading for all business and professional people and their families planning to spend some time in Hong Kong. Authoritative and very comprehensive, it contains everything you need to know from the colony and its future to visas, permits and ID cards, money matters, crime and drugs, the Chinese way of business, festivals, being host or guest, social nuances, and a vast amount of other information.

144pp illustrated paperback. 1 85703 005 2.

How to Live & Work in Italy
Amanda Hinton

Are you planning something more than just a tourist trip to Italy? Do you intend to stay for a longer period, perhaps for business, employment, or study purposes, or to establish a permanent Italian base? Or perhaps you are just considering Italy for the first time as somewhere you would like to spend several months, discovering and enjoying the Italian lifestyle and idiosyncrasies of everyday life? Written by a young English resident, this informative guide details everything you need to know from making preparations, sorting out the necessary paperwork, arriving and getting around in Italy, managing day to day living, dealing with money matters, using the Italian health and welfare system, going to work, doing business, organising school and university education, learning the language, social life, and lots more. Filled with lively insights into the Italian people and their various lifestyles, and packed with essential information, this is a book you will refer to again and again. A teacher and travel writer, Amanda Hinton has herself lived, worked and managed a family home in Italy for the last three years.

160pp illustrated. 1 85703 034 6.

How to Live & Work in Portugal
Sue Tyson-Ward

Do you want to spend some time in Portugal as more than just a tourist? Perhaps you are planning to take a job, study, conduct business, or even retire to this beautiful country? Or perhaps you simply want to go and live there for a while, taking advantage of the low cost of living, and freedom offered by the new Single Market? Whatever your plans, this is the only book on the market specifically devoted to living and working in Portugal; it covers everything from travel and domestic arrangements, arranging employment, house or apartment renting and buying, driving, money matters, education, health care, even to running a business and planning retirement in Portugal. The book is complete with helpful checklists, expatriate case histories, cultural insights, maps, glossary, guide to useful contacts and index. Sue Tyson-Ward graduated from Oxford University in Spanish and Portuguese. She has lived in Portuguese rural communities, studied at Lisbon University, and worked for both Portuguese and English businesses, including the Portuguese Youth Heritage Association. She is now a University teacher of Portuguese language and culture.

160pp illustrated. 1 85703 085 0.

How to Live & Work in Saudi Arabia
Margaret Nydell & Joy McGregor

In the wake of the Gulf war Saudi Arabia continues to offer well paid jobs for a whole range of expatriates from petroleum engineers to construction workers, and accountants to doctors, nurses and teachers. The book covers essential practical topics such as entry requirements, transport, money matters, housing, schools and insurance, plus vital pointers to Saudi Arabian values, customs, business practices and etiquette, providing a complete resource whether you are planning a stay of three months or three years. The authors have both lived and worked in Saudi Arabia for several years. Margaret Nydell teaches Arabic and is also author of *Understanding Arabs*. 'Commendably well written and achieves an unusually high level of accuracy and information . . . Balanced and shrewd.' *Middle East Association Information Digest*.

176pp illustrated paperback. 1 85703 007 9.

How to Live & Work in Spain
Robert A C Richards

Long popular with Britons for holidays and retirement, Spain is now an increasingly important focus for commercial life. Written by a British expatriate who has lived and worked in Spain for more than 25 years, this new book provides a user-friendly guide for everyone planning to live in Spain on a temporary or permanent basis, whether for business, professional purposes, study, leisure or retirement. Written with considerable gusto, the book gives a fascinating warts'n'all account of Spain's variegated lifestyles and how to cope. 'As well as the sort of information one might expect eg work permits, visas, property buying and financial matters, there is so much additional information on health care, travel, holidays, history, geography etc that I feel it would be a good read for the more casual visitor. . . The information is presented in an orderly and interesting way.' *Phoenix/Association of Graduate Careers Advisory Services*.

160pp illustrated. 1 85703 011 7.

How to Get a Job Abroad

Roger Jones

This top-selling title is essential for everyone planning to spend a period abroad. It contains a big reference section of medium and long-term job opportunities and possibilities, arranged by region and country of the world, and by profession/occupation. There are more than 130 pages of specific contacts and leads, giving literally hundreds of addresses and much hard-to-find information. There is a classified guide to overseas recruitment agencies, and even a multi-lingual guide to writing application letters. 'A fine book for anyone considering even a temporary overseas job.' *The Evening Star*. 'A highly informative and well researched book. . . containing lots of hard information and a first class reference section. . . A superb buy.' *The Escape Committee Newsletter*. 'A valuable addition to any careers library.' *Phoenix (Association of Graduate Careers Advisory Services)*. 'An excellent addition to any careers library . . . Compact and realistic. . . There is a wide range of reference addresses covering employment agencies, specialist newspapers, a comprehensive booklist and helpful addresses . . . All readers, whether careers officers, young adults or more mature adults, will find use for this book.' *Newscheck/Careers Services Bulletin*.

288pp illustrated. 1 85703 003 6. Second Edition.

How to Get a Job in America

Roger Jones BA(Hons) DipEd DPA

Millions of people around the world dream of landing a job in the States, despite the strict immigration controls now in force. This book helps you to turn your dream into reality by explaining the work possibilities open to non-US citizens. Drawing on the experience of individuals, companies and recruitment agencies Roger Jones reveals the range of jobs available, the locations, pay and conditions, and how to get hired. The book includes the latest on immigration procedures following the 1990 US Immigration Act. 'Excellent . . . provides you with every scrap of information you'll need when going to the USA to work, from the sort of lifestyle you can expect to job contacts and prospective salaries.' *Going USA*. 'Very good value for money.' *The School Librarian*. 'For young people considering a US exchange or summer employment the section on vacation jobs is particularly worthwhile.' *Newscheck/COIC*.

224pp illustrated. 1 85703 047 8.

How to Get a Job in Australia
Nick Vandome

With ever-increasing competition for entry into Australia and its employment market it is essential for migrant job-hunters to arm themselves with
as much practical and relevant information as possible. This handbook
provides a complete step-by-step guide to all aspects of job-finding in
Australia, for both casual and permanent employment. Where to look for
work, what pay and conditions to expect, and the current economic
climate is explained alongside key information about tax, contracts, your
rights at work and the Australian philosophy of employment; all you need
to know to earn your Aussie dollars. Nick Vandome has himself worked
and travelled extensively in Australia. He has written articles for several
Australian publications including *The Melbourne Age*, and is author of
How to Spend a Year Abroad in this series. 'One book we strongly
recommend,' *Australian News*. 'Very good value indeed.' *News-
check/COIC*. 'Indispensable.' *TNT Magazine*.

176pp illustrated. 1 85703 048 6.

How to Get a Job in France
Mark Hempshell

This is the first book which sets out clearly how to get a job in France,
whether for example in catering, tourism, teaching, computing, retailing,
or other craft, industry, business or profession. We are all today not only
part of a national economy, but a European — and even global —
marketplace; and for those willing to surmount cultural and language
barriers, the rewards in standard and quality of life can considerable. This
most informative book is packed with helpful information and guidance
on every aspect of the French employment scene and will be a valuable
resource for everyone concerned with the growing subject of international
employment. Mark Hempshell is a specialist researcher and author on the
European employment scene. 'Makes a bold attack on the subject and
succeeds in covering a lot of important issues.' *French Property News*.

159pp illustrated. 1 85703 081 8.